MW00764817

The Avant-Garde
RUSSIAN ARCHITECTURE IN THE TWENTIES

ILIA GOLOSOV, ZUEV WORKERS' CLUB, MOSCOW

Architectural Design

Edited by Andreas C Papadakis

The Avant-Garde
RUSSIAN ARCHITECTURE IN THE TWENTIES

ABOVE: KONSTANTIN MELNIKOV, OWN HOUSE UNDER CONSTRUCTION, MOSCOW
OPPOSITE: KONSTANTIN MELNIKOV, SOVIET PAVILION, 1925 EXPOSITION DES ARTS DECORATIFS, PARIS

ACADEMY EDITIONS · LONDON

Acknowledgements

We are grateful to Catherine Cooke who has contributed the majority of material in this issue and has allowed us to use extracts from her forthcoming book *The Russian Avant-Garde: Theories of Art, Architecture and the City*, to be published by Academy Editions. The essay 'Professional Diversity and its Origins' (pp 8-21) is based on a lecture entitled 'Approaches to Architecture in the Soviet Union in the Twenties' given to the Zurich School of Architecture in 1988. Catherine Cooke has also translated the documents (pp 22-31) from the original Russian. The Melnikov interview (p 31) is taken from the contemporary journal *Le Bulletin de la Vie Artistique*.

EDITOR
Dr Andreas C Papadakis

EDITORIAL OFFICES: 42 LEINSTER GARDENS, LONDON W2 3AN TELEPHONE: 071-402 2141
CONSULTANTS: Catherine Cooke, Dennis Crompton, Terry Farrell, Kenneth Frampton, Charles Jencks, Heinrich Klotz, Leon Krier, Robert Maxwell, Demetri Porphyrios, Colin Rowe, Derek Walker.
EDITORIAL TEAM: Maggie Toy (House Editor), Justin Ageros, Vivian Constantinopoulos.
DESIGNED BY: Andrea Bettella, Mario Bettella SUBSCRIPTIONS MANAGER: Mira Joka

First published in Great Britain in 1991 by *Architectural Design* an imprint of the
ACADEMY GROUP LTD, 7 HOLLAND STREET, LONDON W8 4NA
ISBN: 1-85490-077-3 (UK)

Copyright © 1991 the Academy Group. *All rights reserved*
The entire contents of this publication are copyright and cannot be reproduced in any manner whatsoever without written permission from the publishers

The Publishers and Editor do not hold themselves responsible for the opinions expressed by the writers of articles or letters in this magazine
Architectural Design Profile 93 is published as part of *Architectural Design* Vol 61 9-10/1991
Published in the United States of America by
ST MARTIN'S PRESS, 175 FIFTH AVENUE, NEW YORK 10010
ISBN: 0-312-06793-3 (USA)

Printed and bound in Singapore

Contents

Architectural Design Profile No 93

THE AVANT-GARDE
RUSSIAN ARCHITECTURE IN THE TWENTIES

© 1991 *Academy Group Ltd.* All rights reserved. No part of this publication may be reproduced or transmitted in any form or by any means, electronic or mechanical, including photocopying, recording or any information storage or retrieval system without permission in writing from the Publisher. Neither the Editor nor the Academy Group hold themselves responsible for the opinions expressed by writers of articles or letters in this magazine. The Editor will give careful consideration to unsolicited articles, photographs and drawings; please enclose a stamped addressed envelope for their return (if required). Payment for material appearing in *AD* is not normally made except by prior arrangement. All reasonable care will be taken of material in the possession of *AD* and agents and printers, but we regret that we cannot be held responsible for any loss or damage. *Subscription rates for 1991 (including p&p):* Annual Rate: UK only £49.50, Europe £59.50, Overseas US$99.50 or UK sterling equivalent. Student rates: UK only £45.00, Europe £55.00, Overseas US$89.50 or UK sterling equivalent. Individual issues £8.95/US$19.95. Plus £1.50/US$3.00 per issue ordered for p&p. Printed in Singapore. [ISSN: 0003-8504]

Н. ПУНИН

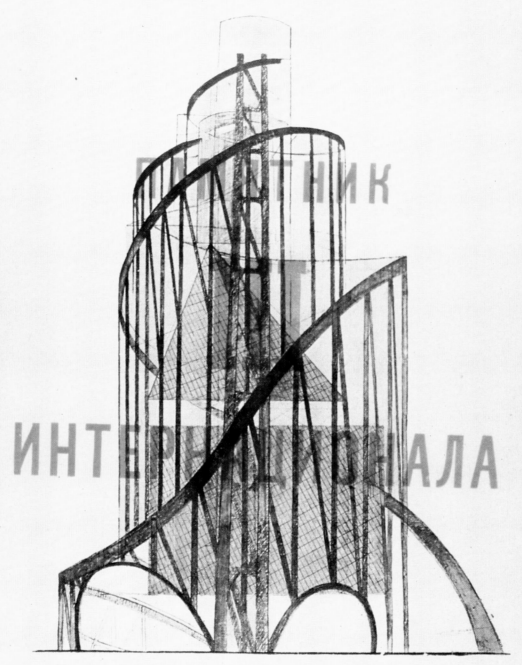

ПАМЯТНИК

ИНТЕРНАЦИОНАЛА

Проект худ. В. Е. ТАТЛИНА

ПЕТЕРБУРГ

Издание Отдела Изобразительных Искусств Н. К. П.

1920 г.

KENNETH POWELL
MODERNISM DIVIDED

Modernism stands divided, torn between social and aesthetic priorities, between orthodoxy and innovation, alternately apologetic and defiant, while its critics brand it as joyless, insensate, detached from popular perceptions and aspirations. A new generation of radical Moderns strives to revitalise the movement, aiming at a synthesis of the forms of the machine and of nature, a dialogue between artists and architects, and a renewed examination of the definition of architecture as itself an art, injured. The very nature of existing cities and towns is questioned, and the ways in which a new urbanism can create a better society are fruitfully debated. Meanwhile, Classicism survives and adapts successfully to social and economic changes. But it all ends unhappily. Supposed 'pluralism' gives way to an architecture rooted in a forced marriage of 'traditional' styles and up-to-date constructional techniques. The 'familiar', the traditional, the well-tried and the beautiful, are reinstated as ideals – but beauty is not the outcome, nor even the real objective.

The scenario sounds familiar enough, though the obvious parallels between revolutionary Russia and Post-Modern capitalist society can easily be exaggerated. ('Moscow Metro' is nonetheless an effect which one of the leading British Post-Modernists admits to striving for). As the New Modernism advances, against all the odds, the history of the post 1917 Russian avant-garde becomes all the more opposite. To the Soviet Union itself and throughout Eastern Europe, moreover, Stalinist aesthetics are being finally consigned to the dustbin. The work of the Constructivists and the other radicals of the 1920s is certain to be reassessed there (and the need for a reassessment is urgent as the East faces the onslaught of facile Western architectural fashion).

'Either build functional houses and bridges or create pure art, not both. Don't confuse one with the other' wrote Naum Gabo in criticism of Tatlin's proposed tower. Constructivism had its origins on the fringe of respectable society, creating agitprop art for the Bolshevik cause. After the close of the Civil War, its idealism was confronted head on by the exigencies of national reconstruction. Gabo was just one of a large number of voices urging the new Russian architecture towards various courses and objectives. But the need of the country was for housing, factories, hospitals, schools and hydro-electric plants, not monuments, however grand the causes they might commemorate. (The scale and urgency of the task tended to override philosophical and stylistic debates. In any case, there was an anti-theory bias in Constructivism,

linked to the ambition of its exponents to abolish the distinction between art and life, between thinking and doing.)

The achievements of modern architecture in Russia were enormous. Yet, to an extraordinary degree, Modernism in the infant Soviet Union was detached from the populace. This was its Achilles heel. In due course, architecture, like every other aspect of cultural life, was subjected to a examination as the Soviet Union sought a popular proletarian art. The outcome, of course, was Socialist Realism – in effect, the rebirth of a conscious style with avowed social and didactic aims and a cumbersome train of cultural baggage.

'Style is not the essence of architecture', wrote Golosov in 1921, 'and what really matters is to distinguish true artistic spirit from style and material values'. Melnikov was adamant that the pavilion he designed for the USSR at the 1925 Exposition des Arts Décoratifs in Paris was not a symbol. In its simplicity, in fact, the pavilion harked back to the genuinely traditional timber building methods of rural Russia. It typified the Constructivist philosophy in its resolute refusal to openly evoke past or present values. Constructivism was essentially a language of pure form – the architect becomes technician. Any symbolism there was contained within the act of construction. Constructivist architecture was, by definition, anti-style and a-stylar.

The fact that style has been so much to the fore in the discussion of modern architecture of recent years (not least in the fruitless 'great debate' conducted in Britain) has led to a remarkable undervaluation of the work of the Russian avant-garde. Lissitzky, Tatlin, Melnikov, Vesnin and others are absent from many of the standard textbooks of modern architecture. This omission was all the more notable in view of the influence of Constructivism on Walter Gropius, Hannes Meyer, Pierre Chareau and, most recently, Richard Rogers. (Lloyd's, in particular, is a striking restatement of Constructivist ideas, directed to the needs of late 20th-century capitalism.)

An excessive concern with form and with theory in the current renaissance of Modernism can only result in an alien and negative preciousness (already apparent in American Deconstructivist circles). This is clearly a case of fighting Post-Modernism on the basis of its own set of rules – more or less inviting the conclusion that 'Modernism is just another style'. An aggressive, socially aware, artistically aligned modern architecture for the 21st century must be based on the rejection of applied style and a Constructivist contempt for applied effects.

Kenneth Powell is Correspondent for The Daily Telegraph, *and member of the Academy Forum Council*

Vladimir Tatlin, Monument to the Third International, 1919

CATHERINE COOKE
PROFESSIONAL DIVERSITY AND ITS ORIGINS

In looking at the architectural avant-garde of Russia in the 20s it is important to see the Constructivists and others within their larger professional context. Too often, all modernist work of the period is called 'constructivist', whereas in fact very similar looking work derives from several quite different philosophies of architecture. It is also quite wrong to suppose that the modernist avant-garde had the architectural field to themselves. The design work of the 20s is also too often presented as if its technical, formal and spatial innovations, as well as its concern with design for the poor, were entirely new features of Russian architectural practice.

In fact much of that progress in these latter directions had already developed considerable momentum in the pre-Revolutionary period. As a result, social priorities of the post-Revolutionary years were more or less agreed, or at least accepted, by the architectural profession as a whole. On the other hand the question of the style in which such objects should present themselves, of the language with which they would most effectively convey the Revolutionary message, was a matter of heated debate. My aim here is to clarify the difference between those various strands of what were loosely 'modernist' approaches, to highlight the fundamental differences of theory behind buildings which often superficially appear very similar stylistically. Some of these approaches are further illuminated here by documents. Others had a clear and distinctive base of theory, but the architects concerned did not develop it so copiously in theoretical writings.

The pluralism of architecture today may help us to understand the arguments on various sides, but the diversity to be found in the Soviet Union of the 20s is not properly described as pluralism. Pluralism after all signifies a democratic acceptance of that diversity as the natural reflection of legitimately different political and philosophical viewpoints. Russian architectural circles of the 20s were no more characterised by such mutual respect amongst the protagonists than Western architecture was in the heyday of the modern movement. My concern here is a positive one, of showing what each group believed about the basis of design. I shall not confuse this by delving into the cross-currents of mutual recriminations and accusations more than is necessary for clarification of the essentials. But the general arguments made against all 'modern' building there are significant, for it was precisely to overcome or pre-empt such objections that some whom we may broadly describe as 'modernists' were already formulating their approaches.

The arguments made against modernism in the Soviet Union of the 20s were remarkably similar to those made against it 50 years later in the West. Modernist buildings were said to be joylessly 'industrial' in mood, to ignore the 'cultural heritage', and therefore not to communicate with the myths and aspirations by which the general population lived their lives. In this there was considerable truth, and Malevich's discussions of the relationship between abstraction and cultural development indicated some of the reasons why.

Even without seeking explanations, it is clear that some of these failures of communications were the result of deep differences of cultural origin between the population and the relatively very small architectural profession, and within that profession amongst the architects themselves, particularly as a new generation rose to greater influence during the 20s. Other disputes were the result of the theoretical battle going on within Bolshevism itself over the proper source of a proletarian culture. The overlaying of these two factors – the cultural and the theoretical – produced the strange alliances which brought the conservative, pre-Revolutionary generation of architects back to the top in the early 30s, as executants of the historicist aesthetic chosen by the new dictatorship. The essence of the argument was already established in 19th-century Russia. In the West in the 80s it re-emerged as modernism versus Post-Modernism. In the Soviet Union in the 20s it was a clash between modernism and an idea of synthesis with the cultural heritage that became called Socialist Realism.

The dénouement in that battle was the competition launched in 1931 for a vast Palace of Soviets in central Moscow, but that it is a saga in its own right on which I shall only touch peripherally here. Suffice it to note here that, even before such a philosophy was formulated with any clarity in the early 30s, there was still a strong current in the profession which believed in the necessity to preserve a continuity with tradition. Whether it was the tradition of local vernacular building, or the tradition of high-art Classicism, both convictions were represented amongst those groups advancing modernist architectures.

As in Europe at that time, the most obvious and direct influence in shaping the architectural theories and aesthetics of the avant-garde was the new art. Before looking at the artistic ideas which formed that seedbed here in Russia, it is important to distinguish the various age and interest groups of that generally progressive front of the profession which in some manner espoused modernism, for the reactions of individuals were very naturally shaped by their personal backgrounds.

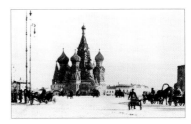

Konstantin Melnikov, own house, Moscow, 1927-29: Melnikov and his wife on site at completion of the brick 'cage', 1928.

Street cleaner and waiting çab-men on Red Square, Moscow, 1912.

Palace Square and the Alexander Column, St Petersburg, during a celebratory divine service, c1900: looking north towards the Winter Palace.

Four Generations of the Revolutionary Profession

Those architects whose offices had been the centres of innovation in the first years of the century were about 60 years old at the time of the Revolution and plainly no longer leaders of change. Progressive free-thinkers like Leontii Benois in Petrograd or Fedor Shekhtel in Moscow became the elder statesmen of the profession during the first Soviet years. Till his death in 1928, Benois was the central figure in balancing stability with innovation in architectural education in Petrograd-Leningrad. In Moscow, Shekhtel continued to be doyen of the profession, remaining President of the Moscow Architectural Society till 1922, and active in competition organisation and juries thereafter till his death in 1926. Some close in age to them died in the upheavals, like Shekhtel's near-contemporary Kekushev, or the Petersburger Peretiatkovich. Lidval was unusual in emigrating to his former family home of Sweden.

Amongst those who lead the new profession forward, we are observing the interaction of what were effectively four distinct professional cohorts. The first and oldest of these had been born at the very end of the 1860s or in the early 1870s, and ranged in age from 40 to 50 at the Revolution. They were well established, in some cases having been through the offices of Shekhtel or Benois, and had built independently. But they retained the flexibility to engage positively with the new situation and to find a synthesis between their established aesthetic positions and the economic and ideological priorities of the new society.

The second cohort were under 40 and had solid professional experience too, but were young enough to seize the new theoretical challenge of the Bolshevik programme wholeheartedly. They became leaders of the main movements and approaches of the avant-garde. The third, whom we may call the younger leaders, completed their training just as the 1917 Revolution broke. They had all the benefits of that solid educational background, but had never built. The fourth and youngest cohort were the first student generation of the Soviet period, taught according to the new curricula which these older men created around the various theories in the 'Free' schools of the 20s, particularly in Moscow.

In referring to these as the 'Russian' profession, not the 'Soviet', I do so advisedly. This progressive core which lead the profession during most of the 20s was precisely Russian. Indeed, it was more against the hegemony of this Russian-rooted elite than against their architecture that the 'proletarian' groupings of the late 20s protested. Most of those who spearheaded the attack on the avant-garde were not bad modernists themselves, but they came from other, non-Russian, republics.

The first and oldest of these four 'generations' within the Russian profession of the 20s were practised exponents of Classicism or the *Moderne* before the Revolution, or famous as innovators with the new technologies. They were part of the artistic and educational elite trained in architecture faculties of the Academy or the Institute of Civil Engineers in Petersburg, or the College of Painting, Sculpture and Architecture in Moscow, to standards rivalling the best in the West of that date. Most had also travelled or studied abroad. Of those who were important in the 20s, the oldest was Ivan Zholtovsky, 50 at the Revolution, who was a passionate advocate of renaissance Classicism and particularly of Palladio. One year after him in graduating from the Academy School was Nikolai Markovnikov, whose career took him to work for the railways and became the leading advocate of small-scale low-rise development after the Revolution. Ivan Fomin was a talented designer equally fluent in Classicism and the *Moderne*. At the turn of the century his Academy training had been broken for several years by expulsion for involvement in student protests, and he visited Paris before working for Kekushev and Shekhtel in the interim. Alexei Shchusev was another successful young Academy graduate who split his career between the two cities and could practice several styles with equal ease. Youngest of this cohort, 43 at the Revolution, was Alexander Kuznetsov. A graduate of both the Institute of Civil Engineers and the Berlin Polytechnical Institute, he had published the first work in Russian on the theory of reinforced concrete design back in 1899 and was well known as one of the profession's most innovative designers of structures and services.

Rising fast beneath this generation at the time of the Revolution was a cohort of architects in their upper 30s, poised to make their mark. Amongst former Benois pupils at the Academy was Vladimir Shchuko, aged 39, with some inventively eclectic apartment buildings to his name, some *Moderne* interiors, much theatrical work, and some fine *Empire* for Russian exhibition pavilions in Italy. Boris Velikovsky had graduated from the Institute of Civil Engineers eight years after Kuznetsov, and already erected several buildings in Petersburg and Moscow. Amongst his collaborators in the latter had been the three Vesnin brothers, Leonid, Viktor and Alexander, who were rising stars of the Moscow profession. Though trained in Petersburg, they had increasingly figured in the prize lists of the Moscow Architectural Society's competitions during the last ten years. Between the Vesnin brothers in age was the Moscow educated Nikolai Ladovsky; whilst the Vesnins became leaders of Constructivism in the 20s, he would lead the rival ideology of Rationalism. Other important future modernists in this cohort were the Moscow-trained Panteleimon and Ilia Golosov, and the Civil Engineering Institute graduates Andrei Ol and Alexander Nikolsky.

Still in their 20s at the Revolution and distinct from this cohort in their lack of building experience, but subsequently contributing equally to theory and practice in the avant-garde, were some highly talented architects born between 1890 and 1895. Backgrounds and education were more varied in this age-group, but strong creative partnerships between these and members of the slightly older group were one of the distinctive features of the profession in the early 20s.

In this third cohort we have Moisei Ginzburg, later co-leader of Constructivism with the younger

Vesnins; he graduated from the Riga Polytechnic in 1917 after a three-year course at the Milan Academy. El Lissitzky's educational career had been very similar. Also forced abroad by Russian educational restrictions on Jews, he graduated from the same Riga Polytechnic one year later than Ginzburg, after a first degree in Darmstadt. Vladimir Krinsky finished the Academy in Petrograd in 1917, and like Lissitzky would later be closely identified with Ladovsky in Rationalism. Nikolai Dukachaev was another future Rationalist leader who just completed his education as the 1917 Revolution brought studies to a halt. Konstantin Melnikov finished the Moscow College in the same year but had managed to get building experience already; like his peers he would soon be back teaching in the reorganised schools, in this case with Ilia Golosov as his older partner. Iakov Chernikhov also belonged to this age-group, but a fragmented educational career put him somewhat outside the mainstream.

These new recruits to the profession of 1917 knew the old 'styles' intimately, as their final diplomas showed. In the 20s they would argue together fiercely over the principles that should generate a modern Soviet architecture, but they were united in regarding it as an essentially new phenomenon, not a reinterpretation of old canons. Within a year of the Revolution their former schools had been reorganised on freer lines by Government decree. Soon they were back there, especially in Moscow, passionately debating their new theories with colleagues from painting and literature in little 'research groups', even as they started teaching the next generation in the studio.

The oldest of this fourth generation were born in 1893 or soon afterwards, and found their higher education disrupted by the hostilities of Revolution and subsequent Civil War. A few struggled through to be amongst the very first graduates of the new era – students like Georgi Simonov who graduated from the Institute of Civil Engineers in 1920, or Georgi Golts and Nikolai Kolli who left the reorganised Moscow school, Vkhutemas, in 1922. In general, however, this youngest of the four cohorts had been born around 1900. Professionally, they were the true children of the Revolution. Their whole training as well as their early professional experience was conducted under the new conditions. It was shaped by the new social programme, and limited by the new economic and technical constraints. The new multi-disciplinary school, Vkhutemas, had been formed by amalgamating the Moscow College with the Stroganov Applied Arts School, and under Kuznetzov such luminaries as the Vesnins and Ginzburg taught at Moscow Technical College, MUTV. From the new curricula here emerged young stars like Ivan Leonidov, Mikhail Barshch and Andrei Burov to join Constructivism, and Mikhail Turkus, Ivan Lamtsov or George Krutikov to join Rationalism. After a period of chaos Leontii Benois's leadership got the former Academy school back to work in Petrograd and in the later 20s its graduates ranged from the formal speculator of Constructive design, Iakov Chernikhov, to the builder of some of Leningrad's best modernism, Rationalist supporter Armen Barutchev.

I stress these age differences because they are fundamental to understanding the differences of emphasis and argument within Soviet modernism in the 20s. Informal teaching, free debate and open competitions enabled young talent to blossom rapidly, but very different levels and kinds of experience were being brought to bear on the problems by people of these widely divergent backgrounds, and this is reflected in the range of approaches.

In respect of kinds of experience, we also have to recognise the different spatial experience brought to urban architecture by students from rural, peasant backgrounds. Most small Russian towns and villages were no more than a loose, low-density straggle of freestanding huts along a broad unsurfaced track. Here as in the wide-open countryside, a building forms a powerfully three-dimensional event, rather than being an object compressed and neutered to accommodate itself to the presence of others. Thus the two greatest formal innovators of the avant garde, Ivan Leonidov and Iakov Chernikhov, brought to architecture a primal, almost carnally brutal sense of form from childhoods spent in the formal environment totally different from the cubic matrix of the European city, which Moscow and Petersburg increasingly resembled, and which their Western-oriented teachers tended to see as essential to a modern urbanity. Melnikov too, though picked up by a middle-class patron in his teens, spent his formative years in that primitive environment and essentially peasant milieu. As fellow professionals these people of very different social and spatial origins fitted in with each other well enough in the melée of the 20s. As personalities however, these three not only retained the fiery personal independence that makes difficult colleagues: their buildings also had in common an independence of form that makes them spatially unneighbourly within the general fabric of the city. The result was a marked formal difference between some of Russia's original avant-garde modernism and contemporaneous work in Europe.

If we consider the origins of architecture's new language, as opposed to its spatial and social dimensions, then we are looking at quite another area of pre-Revolutionary activity: to art. It was Tatlin's early 'counter-reliefs' which first explored the way new materials might generate new artistic form. It was Malevich's 'supreme abstraction' of form in a four-dimensional space-time that provided the formal innovators of many different post-Revolutionary trends with their 'clean slate' for building up a new formal language from first principles.

There is no space here to describe the detailed history of how ideas originating with these artists became developed, sometimes through small scale design work, sometimes directly, into philosophies of architecture. I shall merely outline those stages which help to clarify the orientations of the resulting architectural philosophies, and give references to publications where further detail can be found.

From Art to Architecture
The Revolution of 1917 presented the architectural profession with new briefs, which were essentially concerned with helping to structure the mass

Kazemir Malevich, Suprematist arkhitekton.

Anon, installation in front of the former Muir & Merrilees department store, Moscow, May Day 1921: with productivity statistics and the slogan 'The revolution calls everyone to the great effort of labour'. One of the earliest examples of festival displays on an industrial theme.

Oleg Lialin and Igor Fomin (son of Ivan), installation on the former Trinity Bridge for the 10th anniversary of the revolution, 1927.

population according to the Bolshevik programme. Its main social priority was the introduction of cooperative and collective ways of living that would free women for useful work and make better use of scarce resources, as well as fostering the new political consciousness. It took several years of Civil War to win power over the whole Russian continent and this almost destroyed building materials industries like brick-making, timber-cutting and cement production. Only when they revived a bit in 1924 could any new building be started. Till then, there was no real work for architects: just some exhibition pavilions or street kiosks, small building repairs with scraps of black-market materials. Where peasants could cut timber for themselves there were some new wooden huts. Architects could only dream on paper.

Most artists were busy contributing to public celebrations and propaganda about the new regime. But the serious innovators among them soon started forming into discussion groups and 'institutes' to debate the theoretical underpinings of a new art for the new society. Some of these are very important for the development of ideas in architecture.

The first important year for theory was 1919. In Leningrad, Tatlin designed his Monument to the Third International to demonstrate a new conception of the 'revolutionary monument'. The statement he issued, entitled *The Work Ahead of Us*, was of seminal importance for the future relationship between the plastic arts. The 'functionless' counter-reliefs he did as 'art' in the pre-Revolutionary years, he said, were the 'laboratory scale' preparation of a new formal language through which to respond now to the new society's requirements for material objects. What were formerly 'painting', 'sculpture' and 'architecture' would now become part of a continuum of work with real materials whose end product was functional. From these studies of materials must come a whole new set of 'disciplines' as the designer's tool, which in their different way must be 'as rigorous as the disciplines of Classicism.'

After this very influential statement Tatlin himself did not play a great part in the collective development of these ideas. The action shifts to a group which came together in Moscow in 1919 for just that purpose, of finding a new kind of synthesis or common practice between the plastic arts. Its aspiration was embodied in its title Zhivskulptarkh, literally Paint-Sculpt-Arch, which soon became a slightly more formal research and discussion organisation called Inkhuk: the Institute of Artistic Culture. Inkhuk's programme was written by the now 55-year old Kandinsky, and was a natural development of the ideas he published a decade before in *On the Spiritual in Art*. 'The first part of the programme' he wrote, 'consists of an analysis of the specific properties of each different artistic medium. The point of departure is to be the psychological response of the artist to the property – for example, red is known to excite activity.' This phrase 'psychological response' indicates the underlying focus intended.

Working Groups were established to investigate 'the specific properties' of painting, sculpture and architecture, with the latter group lead by the 40 year old architect Nikolai Ladovsky. His 'work-plan' for the group was

1: the collection of theoretical studies and the existing theories of architecture of all theoreticians, 2: the extraction and assembly of relevant material from the theoretical treatises and from research in other arts that has a bearing on architecture, and 3: the exposition of our own theoretical attitudes to architecture.'[1]

'The painting and sculpture Groups are working in parallel' Ladovsky continued, 'and also the Group of Objective Analysis', of which he was a member, 'where at present it is the principles of construction and composition that are under top priority discussion.' It was from this group that the ideas would emerge which defined the two main avant-garde architectural groupings for the rest of the 20s.

The artists of this Objective Analysis Group, who included the most radically innovative abstractionists, were aware of the emergence of a new creative principle in their work, which differed significantly from the principles in which they had been trained. It was not their abstraction itself which was new, but a more self-consciously programmatic way of creating a form that involved 'building it up', literally 'constructing' it, rather than composing the work as a single perceived image.[2]

For avant-garde architecture in particular, this debate marked a turning point. Those who still believed in the primacy of the old-established notion of 'composition', and still sought to develop the psychological and perceptual direction established by Kandinsky's initial programme, were to become the architectural Rationalists, led by Ladovsky and his colleague Vladimir Krinsky. In 1923, they created the first new architectural association of the post Revolutionary period, the Association of New Architects, or ASNOVA, to propagate this Rationalist approach. The artists, centred around Alexander Rodchenko and Alexei Gan who were convinced of the special importance of the new principle of 'construction', became the First Working Group of Constructivists. The Constructivist architectural group, the Union of Contemporary Architects or OSA, was formed in late 1925 when some of these artist-designers linked up with the architects Alexander Vesnin and Moisei Ginzburg.

ASNOVA and OSA were the two main groups of what we may call scientific modernism. Alongside them were a range of individuals pursuing variants of a more traditional path. Some of this work is stylistically modernist, some of it still historicist. Others adopted various positions in between. I shall look first at Rationalism and Constructivism, then at the most important of these others.

ASNOVA and Rationalism

The work of this group was based on ideas about the psychology of perception, in particular the impact and reading of form. Ladovsky and Krinsky built virtually nothing, but were extremely influential as teachers. The Russian art and architecture schools had been reorganised around the concept of a continuum of plastic arts formulated in

14th anniversary of the revolution, 7 November 1931: procession of Moscow building workers bearing a model of one of the city's new housing blocks.

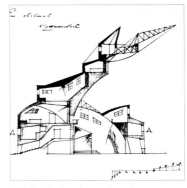

Nikolai Ladovsky, project for a Communal House, 1920.

Vladimir Krinsky, 'Temple of Communion between Nations', Zhivskulptarkh, 1919.

Valentin Popov, Rationalist Architecture studio under Krinsky: Sportsmen's hostel for the International Red Stadium, Moscow, 1924.

13

Zhivskulptarkh and Inkhuk, and most architects of any note also did teaching. Ladovsky and Krinsky were particularly powerful in the Foundation or 'Basic' course at the big Moscow school called Vkhutemas, teaching all students the fundamentals of formal composition, rhythm and expressiveness of form. They also taught an architecture studio, centred on their conception of Rationalism. Ladovsky said: 'architectural rationalism stands for the economy of psychic energy in the perception of spatial and functional aspects of a building', and he contrasted this to 'technical rationalism', whose priority is the economy of materials. On the process of designing, he taught that:

> In planning any given building, the architect must first of all assemble and compose only space, not concerning himself with material and construction. Construction enters into architecture only in so far as it determines the concept of space. The engineer's basic principle is to invest the minimum of material to obtain maximum results. This has nothing in common with art and can only serve the requirements of architecture accidentally.[3]

'The architectural structure of the city', they said, 'directly influences the consumers of architecture by its appearance and by the way whole groups of structures are linked in a spatial system that evokes a particular attitude in the ordinary person'. Thus they declared:

> The Soviet state, which has put the principle of planning and control at the cornerstone of all its activity, should also utilise architecture as a powerful means for organising the psychology of the masses. However, unfortunately, the objective level of development of the humanitarian sciences, the completely inadequate development of the science of art, and the insignificant results that have emerged from modern psychology, do not give us the possibility to fully appreciate that psycho-organisational role which the spatial arts can have in life.[4]

Research in this field would 'give the Soviet architect the possibility to solve urbanistic problems by methods which are inaccessible to the Western architect and planner.'

In their so-called Psycho-Technical Laboratory at the Vkhutemas ASNOVA tried to do such research, with strange equipment for 'testing' people's perceptions of forms under different conditions of vision and movement. Their work was based on that of the German psychologist Hugo Munsterberg. Nothing very concrete emerged to be published, but Krinsky's teaching programme on the basics of form was very influential, and their architecture students produced highly inventive projects.

It is clear here that the Rationalists are more concerned with external form than with details of internal building organisation. The contrast with the Constructivists' approach is already very clear as early as 1923, if we compare Krinsky's project for a skyscraper on Dzerzhinsky Square in central Moscow with the Vesnin brothers' project for a Palace of Labour nearby, both regarded within their groups as seminal schemes. As Krinsky's own

description makes clear, his tower was no more than sculpture: another vertical to balance that of the Ivan Belltower in the Kremlin. Lissitzky's famous 'sky-hook' project had the similar intention of providing points of 'orientation' and 'activation' in the citizen's perception of the 'new' Soviet city.[5]

The Vesnin brothers' Palace of Labour scheme was later described by Ginzburg as 'the first concrete architectural manifestation of Constructivism'. 'For the very first time we see here the embodiment of the vital principles of our new approach to the solution of architectural tasks. This work is uniquely important and valuable for its NEW PLAN' he said, which 'is not the old type of stereotyped symmetrical and ornamental image', but 'attempted the creation of a new social organism, whose inner life flowed not from stereotypes of the past, but from the novelty of the job itself.' The approach to the exterior was similar, with a 'reinforced concrete framework' providing 'a simple monolithic three-dimensional expression of the Palace . . . that flows logically from its internal conception.'[6]

OSA and Constructivism

I have described elsewhere the various stages by which the ideas of Tatlin and Inkhuk were developed during the middle 20s into the approach and specific 'design method' of the Constructivist architects.[7] The most important texts were Alexei Gan's book *Constructivism*, published in 1922, and the writings of Moisei Ginzburg, starting with his book of 1924, *Style and Epoch*, and leading on into a series of theoretical papers in the Constructivists' journal *Contemporary Architecture*, or *SA*, during 1926-27.

It was Gan who first strongly identified the key ideas of Constructivism with Marxism; who drew attention to how the old capitalist buildings were hindering social reorganisation, and therefore how 'correct' buildings could help it. It was he who demanded that Constructivists' 'disciplines' must embrace everything from the largest factors of political principle to the small details of how materials can be manipulated and the relationship between them, and who focused on the problem of finding that correct intellectual logic for the design process which he called *konstruktsiia*.

It was Ginzburg who then pointed to the machine as the proper source for this overall logic. He also saw the machine as a model for generating the spatial organisation of new building types from their social briefs so that they could become catalysts or 'condensers' of the desired social changes. As Constructivists, he said, 'our work . . . consists above all in the creation of a materialist working method . . . which would guarantee us the creation of an integral, unified, holistic architectural system.'[8] Design was no longer to be what Gan had called 'the communication of one's own fantasies.' In a socialist society it was to be an open, collective process to which specialists and laymen would contribute at appropriate points. None of this was to eliminate either the architect, or the role of creativity. As Ginzburg wrote:

> There can be no question of any sort of an artist losing creativity just because he will know clearly what he is aiming for and in

Liubov Popova, detail of her 'construction' which formed the stage-set for Meirkhold's 1922 production of 'The Earth in Turmoil'.

Alexander Rodchenko, 'spatial constructions' of standard timber elements, early 20s.

what consists the meaning of his work. Thus subconscious, impulsive creativity must be replaced by a clear and distinctly organised method which is economical of the architect's energy and transfers the freed surplus of it into inventiveness and the force of the creative impulse.'[9]

The procedures of that working method were described by Ginzburg in a paper in *SA* in 1927.[10] What matters here are its main features, first: that it was a linear process, based on the sort of linear determinism derived from the model of the machine; second: that it tried to embrace every factor which influenced the building task and its context: political, technical, economic, aesthetic.

Every particular design problem was subject to the 'general characteristics of the epoch as a whole'. These were the fact of a collective client and a new way of life; the fact that architecture was part of a larger state plan; the economic need to operate through norms and types; the ideological requirement to operate through 'one single monistic method'. 'Using the laboratory method', any particular design problem was first 'dismembered' for closer examination and then 'reassembled'.

Stage one involved generating 'the basic spatial diagram of the building', which was that 'social condenser', through analysis of the 'flows' and 'needs' of social processes inside it, the environmental requirements, and 'revolutionary rethinkng' of how the technical means available might be used. Stage two demanded that 'the material forms crystallised as the social condenser be examined in terms of the problem of perception, so that the useful activity of the condenser is enhanced by the user's clear perception of it.' This stage embraced topics investigated by the Rationalists, but the Constructivists treated it as only one part of the process of determining building form, not as the most important factor.

Stage three involved more detailed examination of 'the elements of architecture which are the objects of perception: surface, volume and the volumetric co-existence of bodies in space'. It stressed the importance of those 'types of transformation', like cutting holes in surfaces, changes in the relationships of parts or in their material, that offer means of making formal response to a change of the brief. This was the area to which much of the Constructivist teaching about abstract form in Vkhutemas was directed, in particular the serial and combinatorial ideas first developed in the artistic work of Rodchenko. This was also the area explored in great detail by Iakov Chernikhov, in Leningrad. He was not a member of the Constructivist group, nor involved with many of their larger concerns. His work complemented theirs by analysing with particular rigour the 'constructive' formal language which characterises the machine, and exploring its implications for spatial organisation in architecture.[11]

Stage four involved detailed examination of 'the particular processes of industrial production which leave their stamp . . . on individual components and organisms within the building'. 'Re-assembly' would then produce 'a logical building . . . freed from handed-down models of the past.'

'Form is a function, *x*', wrote Ginzburg in a key phrase of this paper, 'which has always to be evaluated anew by the architect in response to changes in the form-making situation.' The mathematical language reflects one of their lessons from engineering: that mathematical precision is necessary in understanding properties of both materials and spatial organisations, and that when mathematics develops further a genuinely multivariate optimisation of form would become possible in architecture.

Given the very short period in which they were able to operate, and the amount of fundamental research demanded before such an approach could be viable, it is remarkable how much rigorous work on these lines the Constructivists did manage to do. By late 1929, the urgent industrialisation programme of the First Five Year Plan put a stop to such long-term pursuits and the whole modernist programme of which they were part. Despite that, the Constructivists' 'functional method' was an important teaching and working discipline that produced some highly innovative design work. In competitions, in work for official bureaux and in student projects, they generated models for many new socialist building types, of which the new 'transitional' housing types were among the most important. Amongst students, as ever, there was a tendency to design 'in constructivist style', rather than pursue the method towards genuine spatial innovation. Others – and Ivan Leonidov was the most important – designed for a far more advanced level of technology than existed in the Soviet Union in the 20s, and was much criticised within the group and outside it. OSA had local groups in several other cities besides Moscow. The largest of them was in Leningrad, and led by Alexander Nikolsky, but they did not achieve much building there.

Other Modernists

The most important of the other Soviet modernists, and indeed the avant-garde architect who actually built most, was Konstantin Melnikov. In Moscow, he is famous for his workers' club buildings, for his own little house and for his city bus garages.

Melnikov was closely connected with the Rationalists of ASNOVA, but only informally. He was not a man who liked either groups or theory. Even less did he like the Constructivists' emphasis on method and the mathematical approach of engineers. The opinions of Melnikov and Ilia Golosov, with whom he taught a studio at the Vkhutemas in the very early 20s, place them in a middle position between the 'scientific' modernists and the traditionalists.

In the statement which launched their teaching programme in 1923 they asserted that:

> Architectural research should consist of the application of well mastered principles of study to the best monuments of historical architecture. Composition, as an exercise in the principles which have been mastered through experience and by experimental demonstration, is the achievement of a matching between creative intuition and the

Illustration from Contemporary Architecture, SA, *no 3, 1926: the engine as model for Constructivist design.*

Moisei Ginzburg, late 1920s.

Konstantin Melnikov, own house, Moscow, 1927-29: finished house from across the street soon after completion.

task posed.'[12]

It is easy to see how Melnikov came to occupy an isolated position. He wrote little but tended to oversimplify the positions of others in order to reject them. In a lecture of 1926 he said:

Most widespread and mistaken . . . is the view that architecture is style, since style in this context means only the sculptural establishment of parts.

The Constructive trend treats architecture as if . . . architectural practice is to be transformed into the necessity to master structural techniques. Since the engineer operates on the basis of mathematics, which is an incomplete science, he can never give complete answers. As a result, engineering will never produce architecture.

For himself, he says, 'architecture is a volumetric and spatial art. It exists as the handicraft act of building, and only the development of this approach to building can produce such forms as we call architecture'.[13]

Perhaps the purest demonstration of this last statement was his own house, based on ideas about rationalising traditional handicraft techniques of Russian building.[14] The descriptions which he later gave of the main spatial idea generating each of his most important designs indicate the source of their power as images. For example:

Melnikov House: EQUAL VALUE AND EVENNESS of loadings, light, air and heat;
New Sukharev market: 2000 small traders ALL HAVE CORNER SITES;
Rusakov Club: THE AUDITORIA CAN BE TRANSFORMED for 350, 450, 550, 775, 1000 or 1200 people;
Dulevo Club: sitting with ANTENNAE in a beautiful WOODLAND;
Model workers housing: now everyone can live in a three-storeyed-complex AS IF IN A FREE-STANDING VILLA;
Palace of Labour project: every person in an audience of 8000 CAN HEAR A NATURAL VOICE.[15]

These concepts represent bold and attractive thinking about the socially new architectural briefs, but the process by which Melnikov arrived at them was entirely traditional. It depended on exactly those chance factors of personal talent and inspiration which the Constructivists believed must be replaced if socialist architecture was to be socially responsive and responsible. Melnikov was unequivocal about this:

There is no obligatory sequence whatsoever for the above processes applied in the initial stages of work on any design. Very much depends on the intuition and what is still broadly known as 'creative imagination'. No work of any kind is possible on the conception of any building, of course, without some preliminary study of the technical and economic features of the task in hand. But it can happen that the spatial treatment and composition take shape in the architect's mind before the detailed work on the economic and technical considerations has started.[16]

Ilia Golosov also asserted that 'architectural form cannot be achieved through knowledge alone. Sensitivity and artistic intuition must also be present. Yet artistic intuition develops through knowledge.'[17] The Constructivists, as we have seen, agreed with that. It was merely their intention that rigorous organisation of the knowledge-based parts of design would liberate the architect's energies for the genuinely inventive part: for making the raw 'social condenser' into 'architecture'.

Like the Constructivists' method, Golosov's theory followed the underlying structure of the 19th-century Rationalists' concept of design, still current in the *Moderne*, where the first stage involved making a crude functional form, and the second stage involved refining that form aesthetically. 'When composing a structure of whatever size' said Golosov,

it is essential to distinguish MASS from FORM. Mass we define as any volume of the most rudimentary kind, devoid of any inner meaning, is not resulting from any particular subjective architectural idea. Being without subjective content, an architectural mass is totally free in the shapes it adopts. The opposite is true of FORM. It is the result of, and is responsible to the meaning which has brought it into existence. To perceive a FORM is to perceive an inner meaning. When a mass becomes invested with a meaning it becomes an architectural form. It is an expression of architectural thought.[18]

Melnikov's design concepts offer examples of what Golosov means here by 'architectural thought'.

When Golosov discusses the principles which are to guide the architect in design, the emphasis is clearly aesthetic:

In analysis of architectural mass and form, one of the highest priorities in terms of perception must go to the principle of MOVEMENT. In every mass or form a correlation of forces expressing this principle of MOVEMENT is always present in some way. Meaningful composition in architecture depends largely on a grasp of the properties of the configurations of masses and forms employed, in relation to their repose or dynamism.

Each structure will have a dominant direction of movement. Achieving HARMONY amongst masses means achieving harmony amongst all the movements. Compositional innovation in architecture finds its starting point in the rhythm of masses.[19]

Here again we see preferential emphasis being given to what the Constructivists treated as just one topic amongst others. The notion of the new aesthetics as a balancing of dynamic movements was a strong theme in Ginzburg's *Style and Epoch*.

Ilia Golosov's most famous design, and the only one built in Moscow, was the Zuev club, where it has to be said that the balance of the forms is more satisfactory from some viewpoints than others. He did an enormous number of competition projects, but his formal vocabulary is much less varied and inventive than Melnikov's. Almost all his designs depend for visual coherence upon a single cylindrical volume juxtaposed to a rather disparate collec-

Konstantin Melnikov, Rusakov Workers' Club, Moscow, 1927-29: view soon after completion; and Ilia Golosov, Zuev Workers' Club, Moscow, 1927-29, corner view, photograph 1989.

Konstantin Melnikov, club for workers of the Kachuk Rubber Factory, Moscow, 1927-29: photograph mid-1920s.

Ilia Golosov, Zuev Workers' Club, Moscow, 1927-29: corner detail, photograph 1989.

tion of rectangular ones.

Among those who must be counted amongst the leading Soviet modernists of the 20s are three other architects of the slightly older generation, contemporaries of the Vesnins and Golosov, who had experience from before the Revolution but were still only in their early 40s when building started again in 1924. They were entirely sympathetic with the new regime, but their less theoretical and polemic approach to the problems of design meant that they still operated from the old established Moscow Architectural Society, MAO.

The most distinguished of these three was perhaps Grigorii Barkhin, who is principally known for his only Moscow structure of these years, the *Izvestiia* building of 1925-27. Immediately after the Revolution he was involved with adapting Russian peasant housing traditions and European Garden City ideas to the new Soviet situation. His approach to teaching and practice was summed up in his later memoirs thus:

> However theoretical, or even at times abstract the problems with which I had to deal, I always believed that both one's analysis and one's conclusions must always be closely intertwined with live practice, and with the urgent concerns of the present moment. As I see it, this is entirely appropriate to architecture which is simultaneously the most abstract and the most practical of all the arts.[20]

This honest pragmatism and balance combined with talent and experience to make Barkhin highly respected in teaching and the profession.

Boris Velikovsky was a contemporary of Barkhin's whose approach was likewise rooted in solid experience of building, but who associated more closely with Constructivists. He had worked with the Vesnin brothers on office buildings before the Revolution, and in his headquarters for Gosstorg of 1925-27 he had three of their Constructivist students, Barshch, Vegman and Gaken, as his collaborators. Continuing where the pre-Revolutionary architects had left off with the boldest of their concrete framed office buildings, this was perhaps the most rigorous expression of a frame and glass modernism actually built in the 20s in the Soviet Union, with interior spaces that genuinely demonstrated the modernist conception of flowing space and multi-directional light which the modern frame could offer.

A man who has to be counted amongst the modernists, though even older and more firmly rooted in eclectic and historicist practice before the Revolution than Barkhin or Velikovsky, was Alexei Shchusev, President of MAO from 1922 to its dissolution in 1930. After graduation he had quickly established himself in Academy circles by scholarly restoration work on ruined provincial churches. In Moscow he had designed new religious and philanthropic buildings in the *Moderne* style derived from simple medieval Russian stone architecture and where appropriate he used more elaborate historicist styles, both Russian and Classical. Indeed it can be said of Shchusev that he was always contextual: he designed in the style that was appropriate to the place and even more, to the time. Thus he declared in a lecture of 1926:

Amongst architects there is a battle for the new ideal, and we shall fight for it unrelentingly. Painting and sculpture have temporarily departed from architecture and now have to justify their presence again. In life today it is primarily economics that drive us forward, and economics is rooted in those same needs which make humanity turn towards building.

Style is not the product of the particular tastes of a few people. Style is a system of how things are decorated, which can be either luxuriant, or poorer. At the present time, we cannot aspire to the luxuriant. We must merely give form to that which derives directly from construction of the simplest of forms. Is this architecture? Does it represent its demise or its flowering? Simple treatments are closer to the latter than the former. If we proceed from the demands of today, we must take account of the fact that right now, the most expensive materials are brick and glass. All contemporary design, based on the simple forms of concrete, brick and glass, therefore shows itself not to be economic. On the contrary: all these aspirations to produce something economic crumble to dust as a result of the high cost of plate glass. There is no way we can talk about architecture in today's context.[21]

In another speech that week he took a more positive approach to the need to redefine the nature and role of architecture, himself preaching that 'high construction costs . . . are why we need a new approach to designing and to the architecture of a building'. 'The architect's ability to solve spatial and volumetric tasks' he declared, could save 'the building technologist and the economist' from just that 'blind amateurishness which our epoch of social change is trying to eliminate.'[22]

Thus Shchusev may be described as a pragmatic modernist. His buildings are generally too lacking in formal and stylistic clarity to be masterpieces. The exception is perhaps his Lenin Mausoleum in Moscow's Red Square. As a leading planner the other dimension of his contextualism was an insistence on the consideration of formal aspects of the site, and the final Mausoleum is unquestionably masterly in that respect.

Classicists

A man whose name is often linked with Shchusev's as a father-figure of the Soviet profession is Ivan Zholtovsky, who was five years his senior. Certainly they worked together as planners of Moscow when it first became the capital again in 1918, and both believed firmly in the traditional principle that any new building must respect its urban context, but otherwise their architectural philosophies were very different.

Where Shchusev could be negatively described as a weathercock, Zholtovsky consistently adhered to the Renaissance design principles in which he believed, and through which he had practised before the Revolution. A brilliant and charismatic teacher throughout the 20s, he considered Renaissance architecture the finest material for training

Boris Velikovsky with Mikhail Barshch, Georgii Vegman and Maria Gaken, headquarters for the State Trading Organisation, Gostorg, Moscow, 1925-27: detail of fenestration, photograph 1988.

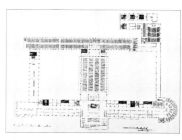

Alexei Shchusev, competition project for the Lenin Library, Moscow, 1928: first-floor plan.

Alexei Shchusev, Lenin Mausoleum, Red Square, Moscow, completed 1930: Stalin, Voroshilov and others taking the salute from the Mausoleum as Red Army troops and tanks parade through Red Square, May Day 1931.

the architect's eye in proportion and composition. He was particularly concerned with the application of those aesthetic principles to industrial architecture, as one of the main areas of Soviet building in the 20s. Several electric power-stations to designs by himself and his students in various parts of the country demonstrated the value of this, notably his own Moges in Moscow, built 1927. The rather flat Classicism of his extensions to the State Bank in Moscow of 1927-29 was perhaps appropriate to its context, but the Constructivists attacked it for 'propagating the ideology of passeists and eclectics'. Equally alien to all the modernists' design philosophy was his insistence on the continuing importance of the facade. However many of the young studied or worked under him to great advantage because of his emphasis on proportion and the traditionally trained eye for balance.

The other important Classicist of the 20s, Ivan Fomin, adopted precisely the opposite stance to Zholtovsky. An exact contemporary of Shchusev, he had worked with leading Classicist architects in Petersburg and *Moderne* designers in Moscow before the Revolution. His Red Doric and later, Proletarian Classicism, were based on a belief that the proportions of Classicism must change as new materials generated different structural dimensions in building, but that the formal elements which expressed the underlying principles of trabeation, solid-and-void etc, remained valid. Where Zholtovsky was happy to abandon columns in his industrial building, for example, but considered the important feature of Classicism to be its proportions, Fomin stretched his simplified Classical elements into entirely new proportional relationships, but believed passionately that the key elements of the formal language must be retained for their inherent 'internationalism' and 'democracy'. In his stripped-down form, Classicism would speak in a voice appropriate to the proletarian state. He presented his argument thus:

The standard and discipline which are so essential to Classical architecture answer in full the needs of our own new way of life, and also of our new constructional practices and building materials, amongst which reinforced concrete occupies a large role.

The repetitive rhythm of the column, on facades and inside the building, are entirely in accord with the uniformly repetitive frame of a reinforced concrete structure. There is no reason to suppose that the joyless look of naked construction represents the ideal of a reinforced concrete building.

Classicism can teach us the appropriate language. This is why it is extremely timely to look backwards, to achievements of former epochs. However we do this not in order to repeat the old. Retrospectivism is not the right path for architecture in a revolutionary epoch. We do it in order to use a decisive and radical reconstruction of Classicism as the basis for our own, new, Soviet revolutionary style for this epoch.'[23]

The Garden Epoch

At the opposite end of the appeal to tradition in the 20s we find those who stressed the merits of dispersed, small-scale development of the type which traditionally characterised Russian towns. We have seen both Barkhin and Melnikov arguing from different points of view in favour of active development of the traditional one-family house, though both of them were principally concerned with the development of a new large-scale architecture of concrete. The leader of the movement which most explicitly continued the arguments and campaign of the pre-Revolutionary Garden City movement was Nikolai Markovnikov, a Moscow architect born, like Zholtovsky, in the late 1860s. Like Zholtovsky he was not only highly experienced, but a teacher of architecture and urbanism who had influence far beyond the circles of those who followed his own particular design philosophy. His relationship with the Constructivists was a typical example of this. Reviewing the first issue of their journal, *SA*, in 1926 he wrote:

If we progress only on paper, then it becomes all too easy to find that we have not moved forward in the direction real architecture must go, but are left aside, or even left behind.

Our front-line practitioners have still not taken note of the already widely pronounced slogan that construction must take account of economics. As a result they produce projects abounding with highly fragmented walls, with protrusions and overhangs, that are economically impossible because they lead to high costs of building housing accommodation.

New forms in architecture can be achieved only through new modes of construction and out of new materials. Both of these will enter our practice with great difficulty and slowly, through the same sort of gradual development that produced such objects as the motor car and the aeroplane. There is no way in which we can foresee the form which the final results of this development process will take.[24]

For the primitive conditions of the Soviet Union in the early 20s, Markovnikov believed in a rationalisation of the traditional low-rise cottage housing. In some cases, as in the Sokol development built to a plan by Shchusev in 1923, some of the houses were built with new materials like experimental types of hollow or foamed-concrete block. Other projects, not built, demonstrated that *dom kommuna* or 'communal house' type of social organisation need not be a monolithic block of expensive concrete or masonry, but could take the form of a low-rise courtyard using entirely traditional small-scale construction.

One thing that Markovnikov shared with the Constructivists was a concern to examine the real properties of a building form or urban layout through the hard realism of mathematics. Thus one of the most important episodes in Constructivism's history of public arguments over issues of principle was the battle between Barshch and Markovnikov over the relative economics of his scattered cottages or their compact integrated housing blocks 'under today's conditions'. Taking into account the

Ivan Fomin, competition project for the Narkomtiazhprom, Moscow, 1924: courtyard screen facing north towards Bolshoi Theatre.

Ivan Fomin, New Campus for the Polytechnical Institute at Ivanovo-Voznesensk, 1926-8: perspective of Chemistry faculty.

Ivan Zholtovsky with Georgi Golts, Sergei Kozhin and Mikhail Parusnikov, project for rebuilding of the Soviet State Bank, Moscow, 1927.

Кроме этого неумолимого закона аэродинамики, — сопротивление воздуха пропорционально квадрату скорости и кубу мощности двигателя, — перед конструктором стоит вторая задача: дать самолет уравновешенный, т.-е. способный противостоять ударам ветра и выходить из любого положения по отношению к земле, если по тем или иным причинам будет нарушен режим его полета. Конструкция самолета, не удовлетворяющая этим условиям, рано или поздно, но должна привести к катастрофе, т.-е. самолет, потеряв равновесие, упадет на землю.

И, наконец, третье условие — метод статического расчета самолета — обязывает конструктора экономить в весе самолета. Из каждой детали выбрасывается вон весь материал, который не служит прочности. Удаляется в буквальном смысле по нескольку грамм материала, если он не несет статической нагрузки.

Таким образом, создается машина максимальной прочности при минимальном весе без какого бы то ни было мертвого груза.

Этот „режим экономии" в весе деталей, которых имеется в самолете до 3500, в конечном результате за счет общего уменьшения веса самолета позволяет взять на один десяток литров бензина, что увеличивает продолжительность полета на 1—1½ часа, или дает возможность пролететь машине лишних 150—200 км.

АРХИТЕКТОР!

И ТЫ УДАЛЯЙ КАЖДЫЙ ГРАММ МАТЕРИАЛА ЕСЛИ ОН НЕ НЕСЕТ СТАТИЧЕСКОЙ НАГРУЗКИ

Короче говоря, три условия расчета при проектировании самолета:

1. *Аэродинамическая форма внешних деталей и их общая компановка, построенная на принципе максимального устранения вредных сопротивлений R_x поступательному движению самолета.*

2. *Наилучшее размещение центра тяжести и сопротивления (R_x и R_y), обеспечивающего максимальную устойчивость самолета в воздухе и*

3. *Удаление из деталей материала, не несущего статической нагрузки,* создают в конечном итоге самолет, облеченный в известные всем красивые изящные формы.

АРХИТЕКТОР, ВОТ — МЕТОД ФУНКЦИОНАЛЬНОГО МЫШЛЕНИЯ

ВНИМАНИЕ

Если просмотреть эволюцию формы самолета от первых его конструкций в период зарождения авиации в 1909/10 гг. по наше время, то с эстетической точки зрения преимущество останется за современным типом самолета.

Первый тип самолета с нагроможденными деталями, с доходившими до нескольких сот метров проволоки и тросса, связывавших детали его конструкции, сейчас уступил место самолету с минимальным числом деталей в форме и с законченностью самой формы.

Эта эволюция самолета явилась следствием эволюции методов расчета самолета, или, вернее, научного обоснования методов расчета самолета. Отсутствие точного знания, в каких аэродинамических и статических условиях работает та или иная деталь самолета, вынуждала конструктора для обеспечения прочности самолета и улучшения его аэродинамических (полетных) качеств усложнять конструкцию излишними деталями и придавать им произвольные формы.

Самолет получался тяжелым, не было законченности в деталях, а сама форма самолета имела вид случайно соединенных конфигураций.

Только современные достижения аэродинамики и аэротехники позволяют в наше время конструктору дать деталь самолета, отвечающую действительным условиям ее назначения и без нагромождения лишнего материала. В итоге получается современная форма самолета, воплощающая идею конструктора, на научно-построенном расчете и в конечном результате — изящная форма, вызывающая эстетическое ощущение.

Эволюция методов расчета самолета за последние 18—20 лет, когда конструктор смог, наконец, осуществить вековую мечту человека — летать по воздуху, — результат исканий человеческой мысли в течение многих веков, и только современное состояние химии, металлургии, прикладной механики, электротехники, термодинамики и аэродинамики, — словом, совокупность новейших достижений научной мысли, а не романтизм или геройство изобретателя, что мы наблюдаем в попытках средневекового конструктора летающей машины, дали возможность современному технику построить самолет.

Строя новую жизнь, создавая ее новые формы, мы кладем в основу научную мысль. Мы достаточно сильны, и наша цель слишком определенна, чтобы современную конструкцию украшать вычурностью и искусственностью красивых фмор.

Инж. К. Акашев

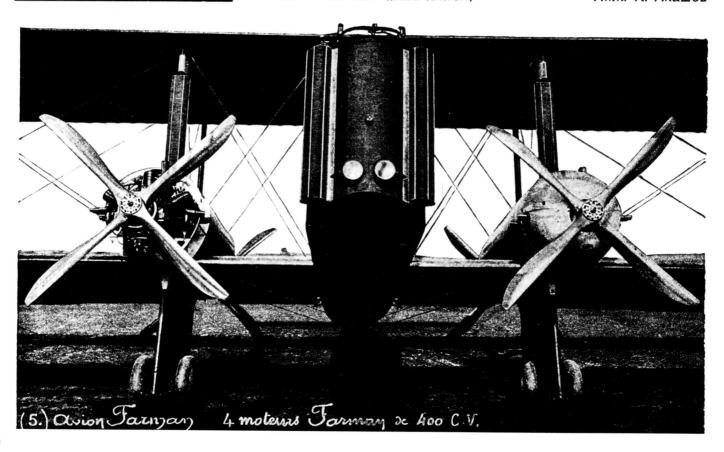

(5.) Avion Farman 4 moteurs Farman x 400 C. V.

prevailing economics of building and servicing, women workers' time budgets, transportation technologies and the collectivist lifestyle, both of them believed that mathematics proved their form the most economic. They differed, however, in the fact that the Constructivists believed that the methods of the engineer would enable the architect to produce a constant series of 'correct new forms' as circumstances continued to evolve and change, whereas Markovnikov saw the lessons of the car and aeroplane as evolutionary rather than revolutionary.

The Soviet architectural profession of the 20s was relatively very small. That was one of the problems of the massive building programme that was launched under the Five Year Plans that began to get going in 1929-30. Collaborator of Shchusev and sparring partner of the Constructivists, Markovnikov serves as an important reminder of the extent to which the key figures, focused largely in the capital of Moscow, were in close contact. The vigour and fertility of the avant-garde resulted not just from the high level of cross-fertilisation and competition amongst themselves, but from the urgency of the situation around them. It resulted equally from the presence within their tight-knit professional environment of this range of quite different philosophies of a Soviet architecture, equally passionately held and sharply argued, and also producing some distinguished and inventive buildings.

The Constructivist design method, page from an article, 'The form of the aeroplane and the methods of designing it' by the engineer Akashev, as published in SA, 1926, no 3, p 66: The slogans read 'Architect! Are you cutting out every gramme of material that does not actually carry a static loading?', and 'Architect! – pay attention: this is the method of functional thinking.'

Nikolai Markovnikov, cottage housing types for Sokol Cooperative Garden Settlement, elevations of a log type and a masonry type, c1923. Full use of the roof as habitable space was not traditional in Russia. This section was identified as angliisky kottedzh, *the English cottage.*

Nikolai Markovnikov, rationalisation of traditional timber and brick construction by reduction of scantlings and storey heights, and use of roof volume for habitable space, 1924.

Notes

1 N Ladovksy, 'O programme rabochei gruppy arkhitektorov Inkhuka, 1921', in MG Barkhin, ed, *Mastera sovetskoi arhitektury ob arkhitekture*, Moscow, 1975, vol 1, pp 345-347.
2 S Chan-Magomedov, Rodchenko, London/Milan 1986 contains transcripts of their discussions. The sheets on which each member presented 'a composition' and 'a construction' to help clarify their ideas are contained in the Western part of the Costakis Collection, see: A Rudenstine, ed, *Russian Avant Garde Art, The George Costakis Collection*, London/NY 1981, pp 110-127.
3 N Ladovsky, 'Iz protokolov zasedaniia komissii zhivskulptarkha 1919' in Barkhin, ed, *op cit*, pp 343-344. The best study of the Rationalists' ideas is, A Senkevitch, 'Aspects of spatial form and perceptual psychology in the doctrine of the Rationalist movement in Soviet architecture in the 1920s' *Via 6*, University of Pennsylvania, 1983, pp 78-115.
4 'Pervaia deklaratsiia', 1928, in, V Khazanova, ed, *Iz istorii sovetskoi arkhitektury 1926-32*, Moscow, 1972, p 125.
5 Both projects were published in the only issue of *Izvestiia ASNOVA*, produced in 1926.
6 M Ginzburg, 'Itogi i perspektivy', *SA*, 1927, no 4/5, pp 112-118.
7 C Cooke, 'Form is a function, x: the development of the constructivist architects' design method', *Architectural Design*, 5/6, no 47, 1983, pp 34-49.
8 M Ginzburg, 'Konstrukivizm v arkhiteckture', *SA*, 1928, no 5, pp 143-145.
9 M Ginzburg, 'Tselevaia ustanovka v sovremenoi arkhitekture', *SA*, 1927, no 1, pp 4-10.
10 M Ginzburg, 'Konstruktivizm kak metod laboratomoi i pedagogicheskoi raboty', *SA*, 1927, no 6, pp 160-166.
11 C Cooke, 'Chernikhov: Fantasy & Construction', *Architectural Design*, 9/10, no 55, London, 1984.
12 'Nakaz arkhitekturnogo izucheniia po programme masterskikh Novaia Akademiia'in, I Kokkinaki & A Strigalev, eds, *Konstantin Stepanovich Melnikov*, Moscow 1985, pp 93-94.
13 'Arkhitektura: lektsii v tekhnikume kinematografii' in Kokkinaki & Strigalev, eds, *ibid*, pp 98-99.
14 C Cooke, 'Melnikov and the Constructivists: two approaches to constuction in avant-garde architecture', *Architectural Design*, 5/6, no 47 1983, pp 60-63.
15 'Sut'riada svoikh proektov – 1965' in Kokkinaki & Strigalev, eds, *op cit*, pp 239-240.
16 K Melnikov, 'Oformlenia proetka', Arkhitektura SSSR, no 5, 1983, p 35.
17 'Aus Handschriften I Golossows vom Anfang der Zwanziger Jahre' in SO Chan Magomedow, Pioniere der sowjetischen Architektur, Wien-Berlin 1983, p 561.
18 *ibid*.
19 *ibid*.
20 AG Barkhina, *GB Barkhin*, Moscow, 1981, p 122.
21 A Shchusev, 'Letskiia: stroitel'stvo naselennikh mest' in Barkhin, ed, *Mastera*, vol 1, pp 170-171.
22 A Shchusev, 'Letskiia ekonomika, technika i arkhitektura' in, *ibid*, pp 169 170.
23 IA Fomin, 'Tvorcheskie puti sovetskoi arkhitektury i problema arkhitekturnogo nasledstva' in Barkhin, ed, *Mastera*, vol 1, pp 129-132.
24 N Markovnikov, 'Novyi arkhitekturnyi zhurnal', *Stroitel'naia promyshlennost*, no 9, 1926, pp 654-655.

OWREMENNAIA ARCHITEKTURA. MOSKAU

VLADIMIR TATLIN
THE WORK AHEAD OF US

December 31, 1920

The foundation on which our work in plastic art – our craft – rested was not homogenous, and every connection between painting, sculpture and architecture had been lost: the result was individualism, ie the expression of purely personal habits and tastes; while the artists, in their approach to the material, degraded it to a sort of distortion in relation to one or another field of plastic art. In the best event, artists thus decorated the walls of private houses (individual nests) and left behind a succession of 'Yaroslav Railway Stations' and a variety of now ridiculous forms.

What happened from the social aspect in 1917 was realised in our work as pictorial artists in 1914, when 'materials, volume and construction' were accepted as our foundation.

We declare our distrust of the eye, and place our sensual impressions under control.

In 1915 an exhibition of material models on the laboratory scale was held in Moscow (an exhibition of reliefs and counter-reliefs). An exhibition held in 1917 presented a number of examples of material combinations, which were the results of more complicated investigations into the use of material in itself, and what this leads to: movement, tension, and the mutual relationship between.

This investigation of material, volume and construction made it possible for us in 1918, in an artistic form, to begin to combine materials like iron and glass, the materials of modern Classicism, comparable in their severity with the marble of antiquity.

In this way an opportunity emerges of uniting purely artistic forms with utilitarian intentions. An example is the project for a monument to the Third International (exhibited at the Eighth Congress).

The results of this are models which stimulate us to inventions in our work of creating a new world, and which call upon the producers to exercise control over the forms encountered in our new everyday life.

VE Tatlin
T Shapiro
I Meyerzon
P Vinogradov

OPPOSITE PAGE: Vladimir Tatlin, model of the Monument to the Third International, on show in Tatlin's studio in the ceramics department of the former Academy of Arts (Free Studios), Petrograd, 1920.
ABOVE: Tatlin, portrait, 1916.
LEFT: Tatlin, 'Corner relief of hanging type. Selection of materials: iron, aluminium, primer', 1916.

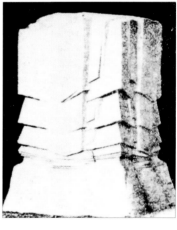

NIKOLAI LADOVSKY
THE WORKING GROUP OF ARCHITECTS IN INKHUK

March 1921

The task of our working group is to work in the direction of elucidating the theory of architecture. The productivity of this work will depend on the very rapid working out of our programme, the clarification of the investigative methods to be used, and of the materials which we have at our disposal, as supplements, in the work. The plan of work can be broken down into three basic points:

1: the assembly of theoretical studies and the existing theories of architecture of all theoreticians, 2: the extraction and assembly of relevant material from the theoretical treatises and from research achieved within other branches of art, which have a bearing on architecture, and 3: the exposition of our own theoretical attitudes to architecture.

The end-product of this work must be the compiling of an illustrated dictionary that defines precisely the terminology and definitions of architecture as an art, of its individual attributes, properties etc, and the relationships between architecture and the other arts. The three elements of the work plan relate to the past, to 'what has been done'; to the present, and 'what we are doing', and then to 'what must be done' in the future, in the field of theoretical foundations for architecture. The commission which it will be necessary to set up for working out the detailed programme must develop the foundations for the programme we have proposed.

The task we are facing involves the study of the elements, attributes and properties of architecture. This is where we must begin the investigative work, on the one hand, with the absolutely central properties of architecture, and on the other, we must investigate those of its properties which because they have a general family relationship to it, have been studied already by other Groups within the Institute [ie within Inkhuk]. Top of their agenda right now is the investigation of construction and composition. For architecture, the most important elements are: space, construction, form, and its other elements follow after that. Here in condensed form is the schema for the programme. But certainly we have no need to confine ourselves dogmatically. For example the presence of results of investigations of questions that are not currently programmed might permit us to deviate from examination of questions in this order. The theory of architecture is a scientific field. And it would seem to require first of all a literary exposition in order to establish its concepts and terminologies with the greatest possible precision. But we must not eliminate graphic representation as one of the means of proof.

It astonishes me that there can still arise amongst group members questions such as 'why is space to be studied as a first priority?'. In such a case would it not be better to turn to our relatives in art, where they will maybe explain to you 'why'. Spatiality belongs exclusively to architecture, but architecture itself does not concern itself with investigating it, and uses it very badly. The dancer or the actor work in space. It is from the theorists of these arts that we must work on questions of space and movement. Petrov touches upon two categories of question: *firstly*, the question of perception (of architectural action). But this is a field of psychology and philosophy. We cannot set up an adequately broad investigation of the question of perception, since we are not adequately competent in the question of psychology. We shall have to limit ourselves here to axiomatic givens, posited by the specialists on these questions. *Secondly*, Petrov, in essence, is carrying out himself a bald classification of the properties of architecture, and not according to its characteristics, but according to purely accidental symptomatic features such as columns, bases, entablatures etc. But what is important in Petrov's words is the once again underlined side of perception and his reference to the University as an architectural product. Would not an examination of this from the point of view of its organic and mechanical characteristics be an examination by analogy. But questions of analogy are questions of aesthetics. There what is being examined is a reincarnation of the individual: where for example a stone lying down calls forth, by analogy, a feeling of rest and a standing stone, an aspiration upwards, and so on. Restlessness, peace and aspiration are questions belonging to a special science, but not to architectural research. And the latter already gives, albeit temporarily, scientifically founded truths, and not analogous comparisons. We are not rejecting psychology, but we say that we are not specialists in it. The same is true with mathematics. But there is a field where we are Pythagorases, and that is architecture. And here we need defined premises to build on. These premises, even if only for today, must be immoveable, otherwise proof is doomed to rapid ruin. Such premises, and directives of a general type, are what our programme provides.

TOP TO BOTTOM, LEFT TO RIGHT:
mid-20s Basic Course under Ladovsky and Krinsky, Space Discipline: three-dimensional classwork on display in the studio.
Vladimir Krinsky, competition project for the ARCOS building (Anglo-Russian Trading Company) 1924.
Krinsky, project for a Tribune, 1921.
Various students under Krinsky, exercises in the manifestation of mass and weight with the subject 'Silicate pavilion for the USSR', Vkhutemas Second Course, 1924-25.

NIKOLAI LADOVSKY
THE PSYCHO-TECHNICAL LABORATORY OF ARCHITECTURE

March 3, 1926

Even if only to an elementary level, the architect must be familiar with the laws of perception and the means by which it operates, in order to utilise in his practice everything that contemporary scientific knowledge can offer. Amongst the sciences which are facilitating the development of architecture a very serious place must be given to the still young science of psychotechnics. This subsidiary science can undoubtedly look forward to a very large field of activity. It has already achieved recognition for itself in many fields of technology. Its influence becomes daily greater, as a result of the fact that it is throwing bridges between so called pure science and practical technology.

Amongst people of affairs the first to have recourse to it were representatives of the vast industrial and commercial companies of America, in the selection of employees, and then trading people used it in the advertising field, and then teachers used it in selecting and determining the capabilities of their students. At the present time there is no field of human activity to which psychotechnics is not making a claim.

In the field of aesthetics the well known psychologist Munsterberg works year by year in his Harvard laboratory. The following studies which have a relationship to architecture have been carried out there: Equilibrium of simple forms (Pierce); unequal division (Anquier); symmetry (Puffer); repetition of spatial forms (Rowland); vertical division (Davis) and so on.

The work which I – and subsequently also my colleagues – have carried out in the field of architecture in Vkhutemas since 1920, verified by the methods of psychotechnics, will help in creating a scientific state-ment of architectural principles on the basis of **rationalist aesthetics**.

The most correct approach to solving this question will be the organising of a psycho-technical laboratory for the study of questions of rational architecture through ASNOVA. To affirm the timeliness of a posing of this problem I can do no better than quote the works of Munsterberg:

Psychotechnics cannot create artists . . . but it can give them all a solid starting point from which they can achieve the aims to which they aspire by the most scientifically correct means and by the same token avoid certain dangers. Through developing psychotechnics across the broadest front, it can in future pose its demands to composers, whilst always affirming that genius will find by unconscious means those things which science works out with great difficulty.

Quite apart from the purely scientific importance which the work of such a laboratory can have, its activities must also have practical importance in everyday architectural practice.

Such a laboratory could eliminate so many of those misunderstandings which arise in the evaluation of qualitative aspects of architectural work as a result of the absence of any agreed terminology even amongst specialists. It is only too well known that chance and accident predominate in the evaluation of competition projects. There can be no elimination of the passion that mutual incomprehension causes between teachers and pupils until the laboratory's work has been set up properly. In these and other cases the psycho-technical laboratory can play a large supplementary role.

Ladovsky et al, equipment for the Psycho-Technical Laboratory in Vkhutemas, 1926: left, Prostromer *(literally: space-o-meter), apparatus devised for 'testing spatial properties of form', above,* Oglazometer *(literally: estimation-by-sight meter), apparatus devised for 'testing visual estimation of volumes'.*

ALEXANDER VESNIN
CREDO

April 1922

The tempo of modernity is fast and dynamic; the rhythm is clear and exact, straight-lined and mathematical. Material and suitability to function determine the structure of an object created by a contemporary artist.

It is unimportant whether the object is useful (*tselesoobraznyi*) and utilitarian (like engineering structures and everyday objects), or only useful (as laboratory work for the task of solving the problem of new contemporary form). Every object created by a contemporary artist must enter life as an active force, organising man's consciousness, influencing him psychologically, arousing in him an upsurge of energetic activity.

It is clear that objects created by contemporary artists must be pure constructions without the ballast of figuration, and must be built according to the principle of the straight and the geometrically-curved, and on the principle of economy with maximum movement.

Since the construction (*konstruirovanie*) of every object consists of an exact combination of basic plastic elements (material, colour, line, plane, *faktura* – the treatment and resultant texture of the surface) the study of these elements must be given priority by the artist.

I view all these elements as materialised energy, as possessing dynamic properties (movement, tension, weight, speed) which must be effectively regulated by the artist.

In the same way that every part of a machine is materialised in a form and material that correspond to its strength and force, to the way it must act within the given system, and therefore its form and material cannot be arbitrarily changed without damaging the operation of the whole system, so in an object made by an artist every element is a materialised force and cannot be arbitrarily discarded or changed without destroying the operation of the given system, that is, the object.

The contemporary engineer has created brilliantly conceived objects: the bridge, the steam engine, the aeroplane, the crane.

The contemporary artist must create objects equal to them in strength, tension and potential on the plane of their psychological and physiological action on the human consciousness, and this must be the organising basis of his work.

Illustration from Contemporary Architecture, SA, *1926, no 3: the aeroplane as model for Constructivist design.*

ILIA GOLOSOV
ON ARCHITECTURAL EDUCATION

April 8, 1921

Study of the styles which have existed in past architecture is necessary. Style is not the essence of architecture, however, and what really matters is to distinguish true artistic spirit from style and material values.

A free arrangement with contrasts and movements is the essence of the artistic process, and content, which must be examined independently from style and which in essence can adopt any specific form, is entirely independent of style. Thus the study of style does not offer a path to understanding the essence of architecture. That is why it should not be seen as part of the course of study of architectural structures.

The study of traditional architecture must undoubtedly enter into the programme of teaching on architecture but under no circumstances should it be taught on the level of its external appearances as style. It should aim to convey an understanding of its essence: of the principles for building up masses; of the placing of masses and of the ways of perceiving them; of the relationship of plans to elevations; and of functional suitability of form.

This is the only viewpoint from which historical architecture should be examined in a foundation course of architectural design. They should have been given the necessary factual information on the classics of architecture and such topics as the orders in advance, through conventional lecture courses of the kind used in all architectural schools as the main means for teaching classical proportions in particular.

The study and knowledge of proportions as such is necessary in the early part of architectural education, but must not be based exclusively on the examples of the classics. In these artistic works which constantly repeat the same overall structure, as do Greek temples for example, students can work out for themselves the more or less constant relationships of different parts of the building. But in the study of proportions in general, we must not be led only by those principles, since the sets of proportions necessary for certain given kinds of design work must be created afresh. They cannot always conform to a definition of the relationship of elements that has been established once and for all time.

I consider that the programme which has currently been accepted for the basic course of architectural study does not satisfy the above mentioned principles, therefore I propose to replace architectural drafting exercises by the study of how architectural form is structured, in accordance with the following schema:

Programme for conducting architectural training in the First Course:

1　General concepts of architecture, its tasks, and its significance in the life of humanity.
2　The architectural mass:
　　The concept of architectural mass.
　　The placing of masses.
　　The relationship of masses.
　　The scalar qualities of masses.
3　Architectural form:
　　The concept of architectural form.
　　How form depends on content.
　　The relationship of forms.
　　The scalar qualities of form.
　　Composition of simple architectural structures in terms of their plan, elevations and sections.
4　The architectural treatment of masses and forms:
　　The significance of a different architectural treatment of one and the same mass.
　　The manifestation of scale in a mass through the treatment of its parts as architectural details.
5　Means of expression:
　　Manifestation of the powerfulness of a building.
　　Manifestation of the grace of the building.
　　Manifestation of the idea of the building.
　　Compositions of a simple piece of monumental architecture showing plan, elevations and sections.
6　The significance of spatial relationships.
7　Rhythm in architecture.

Ilia Golosov, Zuev workers' club, Moscow 1927-29: plans of the four main levels.

ILIA GOLOSOV
NEW PATHS IN ARCHITECTURE

December 13, 1922

In recent times we can observe a certain trend of aesthetic thinking in the architectural world, which expresses itself mainly and principally in a negative attitude to classical architectural forms as possible models for the present time. We are seeing the search for new forms, more suitable for our own age.

We architects of today have too long been the slaves of the classics, and for too long have forgotten that the forms of social life, the customs and beliefs of the peoples of our age are in no way similar to those of previous historical epochs. There is therefore no basis for proposing a reuse of ancient historical forms for the future, because repetition of that which is outlived, in art of today or of the future, can only destroy its rationality and its suitability to purpose.

In respect of our creative principles, our many centuries of slavery have stamped us with inactivity. We live as it were outside time – outside contemporary life. Its current is flowing past us. The grandiose structures of our time are being erected whilst we look on. Life is moving forward with gigantic steps, requiring of art, as of architecture, that it fulfil its purpose. Everything is embraced by the flow of life, everything lives in time and there is no place in progress for those who are deaf to the living impulse of the community and who exist outside time.

If architecture is seen as the art of making contemporary aesthetic forms accessible to all, of embodying almost all the other forms of art within itself, then contemporary architecture is in a very sad state. In essence, it does not exist at all. There is only the imitation of classical architecture trying to express itself in contemporary buildings. We architects, as active people in our field, have not up till now been creators of new forms organically connected with the present epoch. We were reproducers of classical forms and proportions which were essentially alien to us but have become a symbol of truth for the contemporary architect and represent his only source of inspiration.

I am not inclined to insist however that classic and historical forms in architecture are absolutely negative for our time and that application of them now is always an absurdity, but I am convinced it is unarguable and urgently necessary to establish the degree to which these forms are applicable in the buildings of our time.

It is obvious that classical forms may be applied to the extent that they incorporate fundamental principles which have absolute validity for all time. Thus the column as a supporting pillar remains a basic element in building. So too do the arch and the vault, or the pediment as a result of a double-pitched roof, and so on. Whilst buildings utilise those constructional elements, the forms will retain a validity. However it is always necessary to distinguish the form which is an aesthetic expression of something constructive, from forms which are merely abstracted or decorative elements.

In this country we possess a great example of how the application of antique forms in architecture can be avoided. That example is given us by the old buildings of the Russian people. Despite the fact that classicism was dominant in Europe during the period when the Russian people were creating their architecture, and despite the influence of Western culture on the whole fabric of life here, Russia created architectural forms that were entirely distinct from those of classicism, under the influence of her own way of life.

Russian historical churches have forms that are absolutely unique, which are structured, however, according to eternally unchanging laws of the aesthetic structuring of masses in space. Herein consists the main aesthetic value of what the Russian people created in its great periods of building.

Russian culture was gradually displaced by that of the West, and to the extent that the latter became established on our soil, Russian people like their Western neighbours became slaves to classical forms.

An individual quickly spots the easy victory and follows such a path at the first opportunity. Thus the Russian people lost their aesthetic individuality and everything hard-won by their own great intuition and invention was thrown to the winds. The values incorporated in the products of their own creativity were thrown to the mercy of fate as they starting rolling down the slope of easily-won, irresponsible achievements.

The architecture of the present and the future cannot be built upon slavery and subordination to the history of art. Life demands of us, contemporary architects, an altogether more fruitful activity in the spirit of our own time. It demands products in full accord with the technology and the social structure of life today.

What then are the requirements that must be made of the contemporary architect? Above all he must so create artistic forms that they respond to the place, the time, and the spirit or idea of the thing which is being created. The architect must be freed from style, in the old sense of the word, and must himself create the style which emerges as a result of a correspondence between the architectural forms and the content or purpose, the idea, which they serve.

We should not be working for the applause of the crowds, but for the serious evaluation of our activity. We must be working to achieve a solid basis for our work in principles that can become the foundations for the renaissance of architecture that is meaningful and expressive, in harmony with its epoch. We should not be actors-out of historical architecture, but creators of forms that are rational for the age in which they arose.

KONSTANTIN MELNIKOV
FROM LECTURES TO THE ACADEMY OF MILITARY ENGINEERS

November 1923

I draw your attention to one principle which is purely architectural, and is self-evident in its definition, namely this: any building, in producing an impression of some kind on us, will have a greater effect of surprise on our feelings if we perceive that its actual dimensions are far smaller than our impression lead us to believe. That is what one might call an artistic illusion of the parts of the building, and is achieved not through rhythmic combination of those parts, but mainly by an aesthetic concept underlying the design. The questions are interesting, but difficult to define. There are a great number of these aesthetic rules, and each epoch has its own; indeed in any given epoch the rules differ between different peoples and nations, and are often in contradiction with each other. I shall talk about those things that are not matters of argument in aesthetics, which can be demonstrated and can be physically felt.

Looking at a column from the Parthenon, I draw your attention to one detail in particular: the flutes. Each flute has an outward circular continuation whose measure is unquestionably greater than that of the column's diameter, that is than the line defining the body of the column. Thanks to this the column seems fatter than its real size. By their vertical upward movement these flutes also strengthen the column's verticality. Thus on the one hand it seems that the column is fatter than it really is, on the other hand, it seems taller. This aesthetic device imparts to the column a fascinating harmoniousness.

We come to the enlargement of volume by planes. This device is to be seen in at every step in the great historical monuments of architecture. In this respect, creative imagination is not confined to any single geometrical structure.

In the famous caryatids of the Temple of the Erechtheion we see columns replaced by the figures of women. For centuries the sculptural pediments of the Parthenon have served as sources of imitation for this same device: the introduction of sculptural form has an effect on the impression we receive, giving greater overall strength to the form of the building. The pleasant impression we get from the vaults of Rome, Byzantium and the medieval period is explained by this same law: that the curved surface is larger than the straight one, and therefore the space which is covered by it seems to be larger.

This aesthetic rule, with its possibility for physical calculations of the image reinforcement achieved, was familiar and well studied in Ancient Egyptian.

The Great Pyramids of Cheops produces its stunning impression by the grandiose dimensions of a) its volume (the quantity of materials): b) its perimeter; c) its area, its surface; d) its height relative to its cubic volume.

Amongst contemporary works in which this same principle applies, I draw your attention to the building I myself constructed in 1925 in Paris, at the International Exhibition of Decorative Arts. The site we were allocated was extremely small. Its overall dimensions were a mere 11m by 29.5m. In order to enlarge it, I took the diagonal as the main axis of the architectural composition, this being the longest dimension in the rectangle.

I would further draw your attention to the design of the staircase. It is not broad, but because it is on the skew it seems very large and ceremonial. I would also point out that as a result of this device, it turned out that the shifted volumes of the interior space also worked on the elevation, by in fact enlarging the number of square meters of wall on the facade. The roof too was fragmented into elements, and overall this structure of small physical dimensions had the appearance of a large celebratory building. The effect was enhanced by the spatial mast with its red flag, which announced its presence to the whole exhibition.

Konstantin Melnikov, own house, Moscow, 1927-29: plans, left to right, ground, first and mezzanine floors.

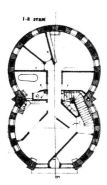 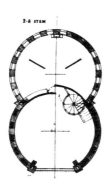 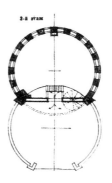

KONSTANTIN MELNIKOV
USSR PAVILION
Exhibition of Decorative Arts, Paris 1925

Summer 1925

Interviewer: Please tell us in more detail about your pavilion. What is the basic idea behind it?

Melnikov: This glazed box is not the fruit of an abstract idea. My starting point was real life; I had to deal with real circumstances. Above all, I worked with the site that was allocated to me, a site surrounded by trees: it was necessary that my little building should stand out clearly amidst the shapeless masses through its colour, height and a skilful combination of forms. I wanted the pavilion to be as full of light and air as possible: that is my personal predilection and I think it reasonably represents the aspiration of our whole nation. Not everyone who walks past the pavilion will go inside it. But each of them will all the same see something of what is exhibited inside my building, thanks to the glazed walls, and thanks to the staircase which goes out to meet the crowd, passes through the pavilion and enables them to survey the whole of its content from above. As far as the intersecting diagonal planes over the route are concerned, may they be a disappointment to lovers of roofs corked up like bottles! But this roof is no worse than any other: it is so made as to let in the air, and you keep out the rain from whatever direction it may fall.

Interviewer: But don't you think that all this glass and this strange roof make your pavilion much too lightweight?

Melnikov: You are really saying that you would prefer something more heavyweight. But why should a building whose function is temporary be given false attributes of the everlasting? My pavilion doesn't have to keep standing for the whole life of the Soviet Union. It is quite enough for it to keep standing until this exhibition closes. To put it briefly, the clarity of colour, the simplicity of line, the abundance of light and air which characterise this pavilion, whose unusual features you may like or dislike according to taste, have a similarity to the country from which I come. But do not think, for goodness sake, that I set out to build a symbol.

Konstantin Melnikov, Soviet Pavilion at the Exposition des Arts Décoratifs, Paris, 1925: competition project, 1924, elevation. The complex plan had a circular element extreme left, and the entrance route divided about a pedestal with statue of Lenin, right, obscured in this view.

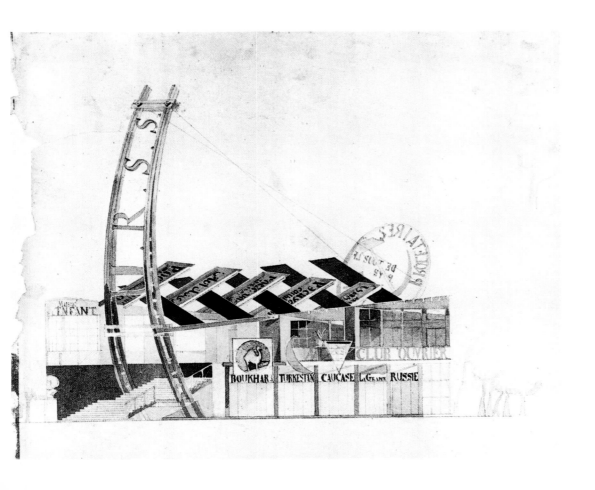

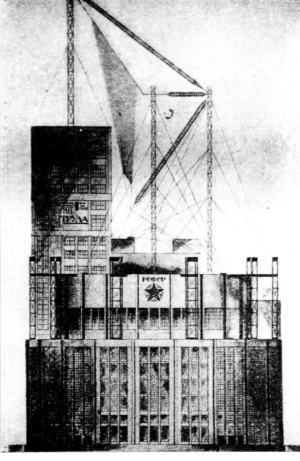

Rationalism/Constructivism Compared
Building Projects – 1923

a: Vladimir Krinsky, *skyscraper headquarters for the Supreme Soviet of the National Economy (Vesenkha USSR), Lubianka (now Dzerzhinsky) Square, 1923: photomontage from model.*
b, c: Vesnin Brothers, *competition project for the Palace of Labour, Moscow, 1923: perspective, elevation.*
d, e: Vladimir Krinsky, *skyscraper headquarters for the Supreme Soviet of the National Economy, notional plans with partial elevation to Square modelled in relief, side elevational drawing.*
f: Volodko, *project for Vesenkha skyscraper: in montage with (inverted) Ivan Belltower of the Kremlin, illustrating role of Vesenkha tower as a second vertical in the central Moscow skyline.*
g: Vesnin Brothers, *Competition project for the Palace of Labour, plans.*

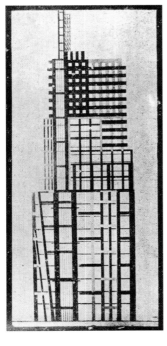

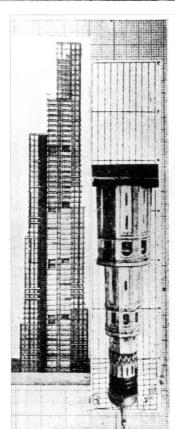

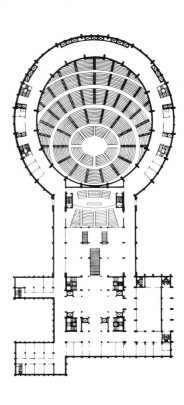

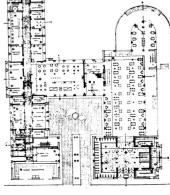

*a: Armen Barutchev, Isidor Gilter,
Iosif Meerson and Iakov Rubanchik,*
factory kitchen and public feeding
complex for the Viborg district of
Leningrad, 1929-30: photograph soon
after completion.
b, c: ground-floor plan, section.
d: entrance elevation, photograph
1989.
e: axonometric drawing.
f: perspective drawing.
*g: Barutchev, Gilter, Meerson,
Rubanchik,* factory kitchen and
public feeding complex for Vasily
Island, Leningrad, 1930-31:
northwest elevation, photograph
1989.
h: southeast corner, with semi-
circular dining hall in trees, right,
photograph 1989.

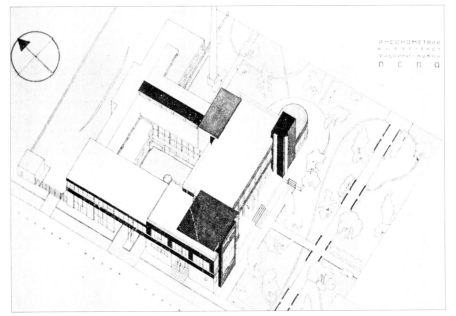

a: *Armen Barutchev, Isidor Gilter,*
Iosif Meerson and Iakov Rubanchik,
department store, factory kitchen and
public feeding complex for the Kirov
district of Leningrad, 1929-31:
perspective, preliminary version.
b: *daytime photograph soon after*
completion.
c: *night view soon after completion.*
d: *illuminated model of final design,*
with department store, left, and
feeding accommodation, right.
e: *view towards main entrance of*
feeding complex with department
store beyond, photograph 1989.
f: *semi-circular dining hall with*
central servery, photographed without
furniture.
g: *view along shop front from*
entrance to feeding section.
h: *semi-circular dining room, evening*
view looking towards windows.

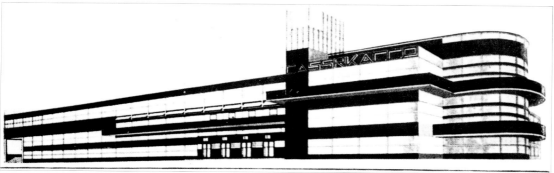

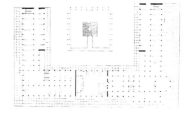

a, b: Daniil Fridman, 5th prize-winning competition project for the House of Government in Alma-Ata, 1927: perspective, first-floor plan.
c: Dimitri Markov, Daniil Fridman, Vladimir Fidman, competition project for the Lenin Library, Moscow, 1928, first stage: perspective.
d: second stage: perspective.
e, f: Andrei Bunin, Liubov Zalesskaia, Maria Kruglova, Mikhail Turkus et al, Competition project for the State Theatre of Massed Musical Activities, Kharkov, 1930: photograph of model, plans.
g: Markov, Fridman, Fidman, Lenin Library Competition, second stage: ground-level plan.

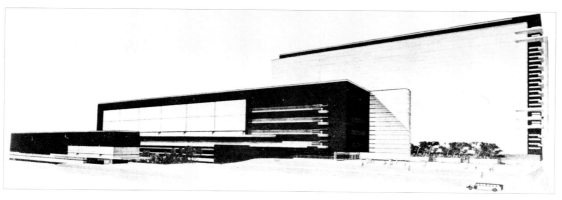

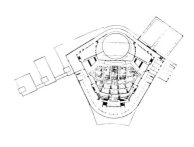

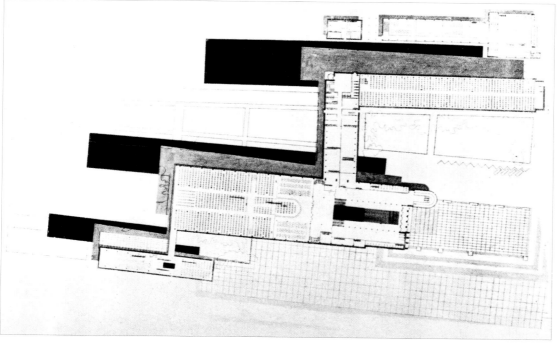

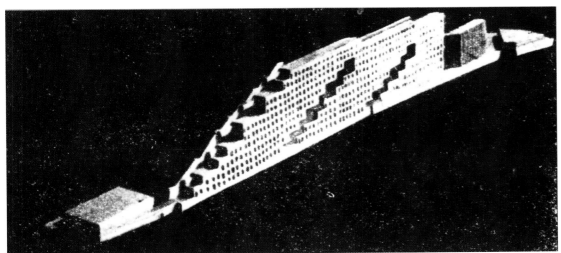

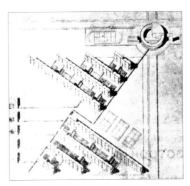

a, b: Viktor Kalmykov, 'housing combine' of 700 and 1000 people, for the new city of Avtostroi.
c: Vitaly Kaplun, 'housing combine' for the new city of Avtostroi.
d: Georgi Krutikov, Vitaly Lavrov and Valentin Popov, competition project for the new city of Avtostroi, 1930: part of the housing district, with sleeping blocks and circular social facilities building.
e: central strip with public buildings.
f: general view of model.
g: axonometric of communal housing blocks.
h: view of the city from the inter-urban highway.

город-коммуна АВТОСТРОЙ

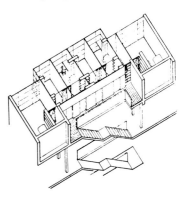

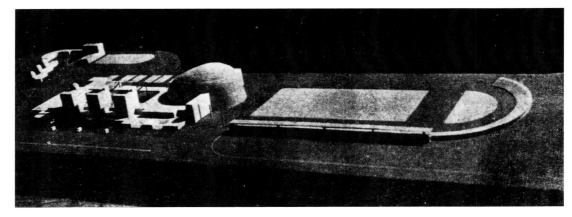

ДВОРЕЦ КУЛЬТУРЫ

АСНОВА

40

ПАРАБОЛИЧЕСКИЙ ДОМ

А. БУНИН

a, b: Unidentified ASNOVA teams, competition projects for a Palace of Culture beside the Moscow River, 1930: photographs of the models.
c: Nikolai Ladovsky, passenger entrance to the Red Gates metro station, 1934-35: photograph 1985.
d, e: Andrei Bunin, parabolic tower as solution to the problem of urban housing in the northern climate, 1930: elevation, model.
f, g: section, perspective under towers.
h: second-floor plan.

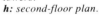

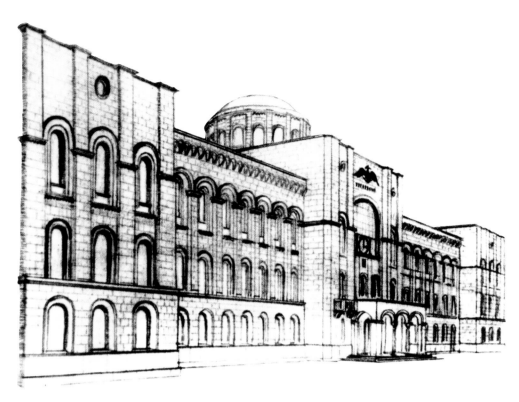

Buildings by OSA Members – Vesnin Brothers

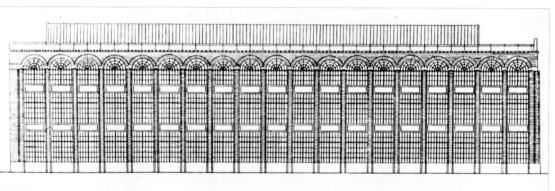

a: Vesnin Brothers, for the office of OR Munts, Facade of the Moscow Central Post Office, 1911: perspective.
b: Leonid Vesnin, project for a dacha, 1908: perspective.
c: Vesnin Brothers, weaving shop for Tomna Plant in Great Kineshemskaia, 1916-17: elevation.
d: Competition project for the Gostinyi Dvor (retail shopping centre), Nizhni-Novgorod, 1914: perspective.
e: Leonid Vesnin with VA Simov, dacha for VA Nosenskov in Ivankovo near Moscow, 1909-11: contemporary photograph.

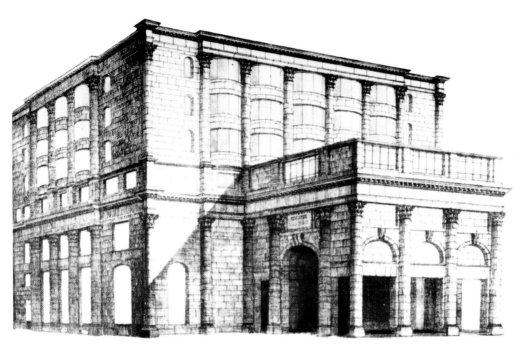

a: Vesnin Brothers, development project for Mr. Roll, Moscow, 1913: perspective of the hotel.
b: Mansion for DV Sirotkin in Nizhni-Novgorod, 1915-16: perspective.
c: Project for the Dinamo company's department store, Moscow, 1916-17: perspective.

a: Viktor Vesnin, Chernorecheskii super-phosphate plant in Nizhni-Novgorod, 1918-19: perspective.
b: Alexander Vesnin, stage set for GK Chesterton's play 'The Man who was Thursday', Kamerny Theatre, Moscow, 1923.
c: Vesnin Brothers, natural turpentine plant near Kostroma, 1922-24.

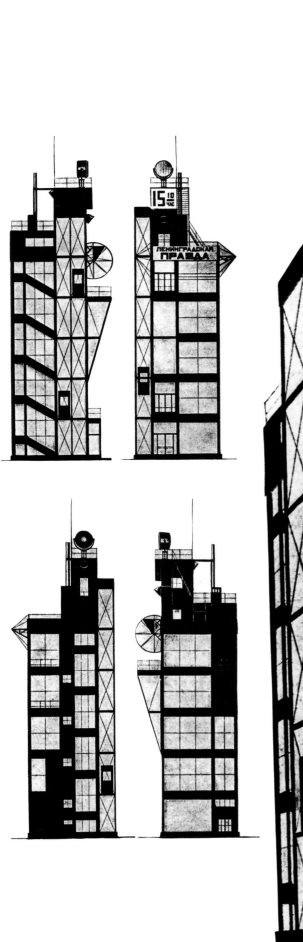

a: Vesnin Brothers, *competition project for Moscow offices of the newspaper* Leningradskaia Pravda, *1924: four elevations.*
b: *perspective.*
c, d: *first and ground-floor plans.*

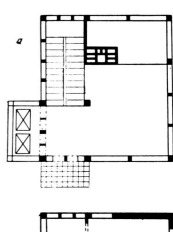

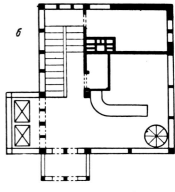

В. А. ВЕСНИН. ИВСЕЛЬБАНК
W. WESNIN. DIE BANK ZU IWANOWO-WOSNESSJENSK

*a: Vesnin Brothers, Mostborg
department store, Krasnaia Presnia,
Moscow, 1927: photograph of
entrance, 1928.
b: photograph of front, 1928.
c: Viktor Vesnin, Ivselbank Agricultural Bank, Ivanovo-voznesensk,
1927: perspective and photograph
during construction.
d: Viktor Vesnin, Institute of Mineral
Raw Materials for the Scientific
Section of Vesenkha, Moscow, 1925:
general view during construction.
e: view across the flat roofs.*

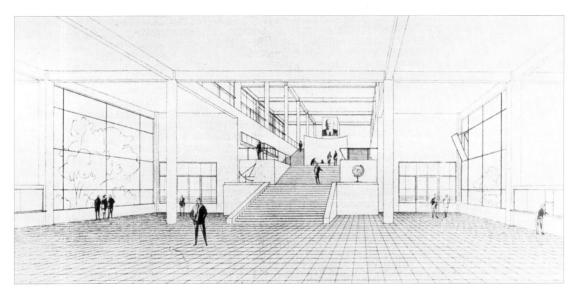

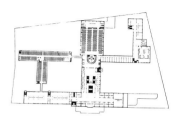

a: Vesnin Brothers, *competition project for the Lenin Library, Moscow, second variant, 1928: perspective of main entrance hall.*
b, c: *ground and first-floor plans.*
d: *Workers' club at Bailov in Baku, 1928: perspective.*
e: *Competition project for the Lenin Library, perspective.*
f: *Club for the Society of Former Political Prisoners of Tsarism, Moscow, 1931-35: detail with entrance steps, photograph 1987.*
g: *perspective (building only partially executed).*

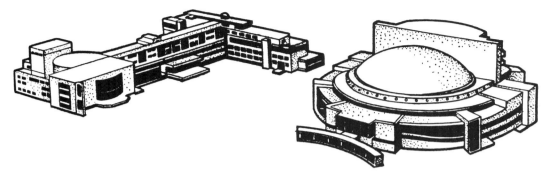

a: Vesnin Brothers, Palace of Culture
of the Proletarsky district of Moscow,
1931-37: isometric drawing of the
whole complex (theatre, right, not
built).
b: main entrance to foyers and
auditorium, photograph, 1987.
c: entrance to Winter Garden with
observatory dome over photograph,
1987.
d: first-floor foyer, photograph of the
1930s.

АРХИТЕКТОР!

ТАК НУЖНО ПОНИМАТЬ МА-
ТЕРИАЛИСТИЧЕСКИЕ ОСНОВЫ
ЭСТЕТИКИ КОНСТРУКТИВИЗМА

*a: **Moisei Ginzburg,** competition
project for the Palace of Labour,
Moscow, 1923: perspective of main
entrance.*
*b: Competition project for the House of
Textiles, Moscow, 1925: section
showing courtyard and vehicle ramps
to carparking below.*
c: perspective.
*d-f: floors 7 & 8, floor 9, plans of
basement carpark.*

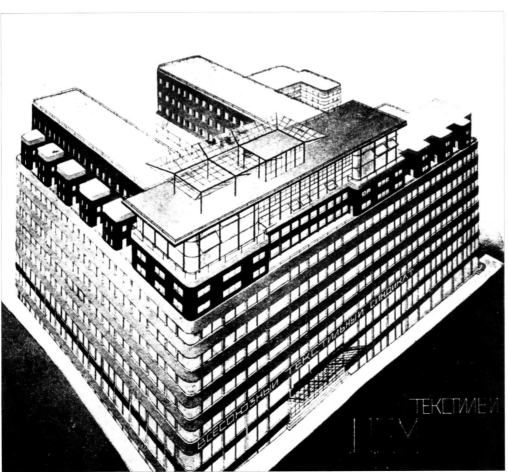

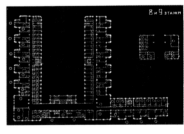

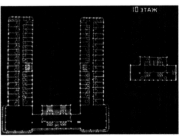

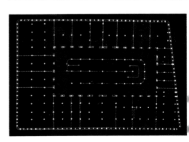

a: Moisei Ginzburg, Apartment and
communal housing block for the State
Insurance Bureau, Gostrakh, built
1926-27: street view.
b, c: view of roof terrace from adjacent
building, photograph 1927: axonometric.

НОВЫЕ МЕТОДЫ
АРХИТЕКТУРНОГО МЫШЛЕНИЯ

a: **Moisei Ginzburg**, *apartment and communal housing block for the State Insurance Bureau, Gostrakh, Moscow, built 1926-27: upper corner, from street, photograph 1927.*
b: *typical floor plan.*
c: *Ginzburg enjoying his Moscow* toit jardin, *1927.*
d: *space-saving folding* couchette *('Cupboard-bed').*

НОВЫЕ МЕТОДЫ
АРХИТЕКТУРНОГО МЫШЛЕНИЯ

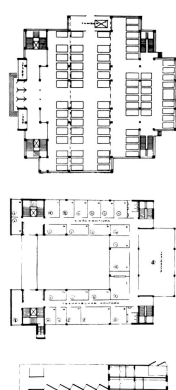

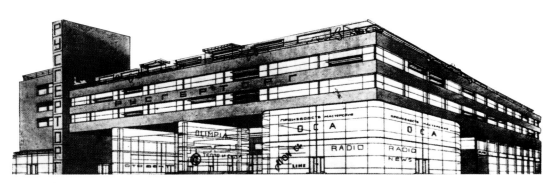

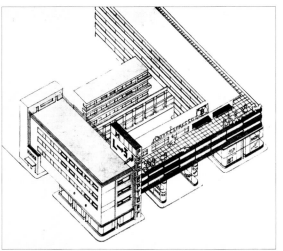

a: Moisei Ginzburg, competition project for the Orgamental Headquarters, Moscow, 1926: perspective.
b-d: section, showing central top-lit space, plan of second and third floors, with offices and drawing office, ground-floor plan, showing exhibition space for orgamental machines.
e, f: Moisei Ginzburg with V Vladimirov and A Pasternak, competition project for headquarters of the Russo-German Trading Company, Russgertorg, Moscow, 1926: perspective, isometric.

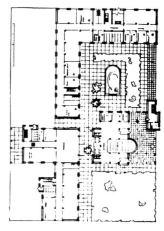

a, b: Moisei Ginzburg with I Milinis, *competition project for the House of Government of the Kazakh Republic, Alma-Ata, 1928 (first prize: built 1929-31): axonometric and ground plan.*
c: *cutaway axonometric view of bridge 'court' and rear of auditorium.*
d, e: *first and second-floor plans.*

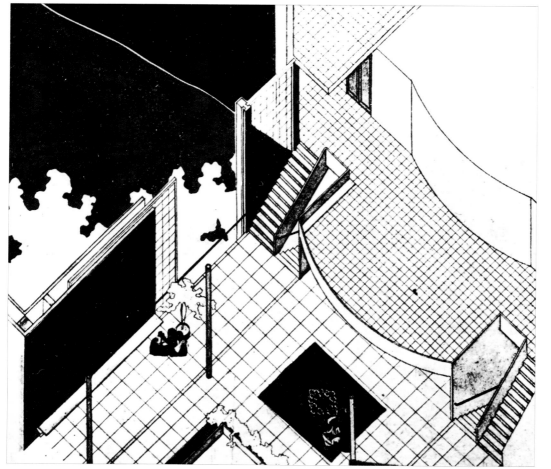

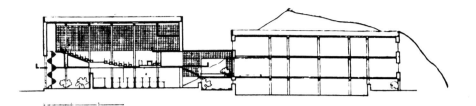

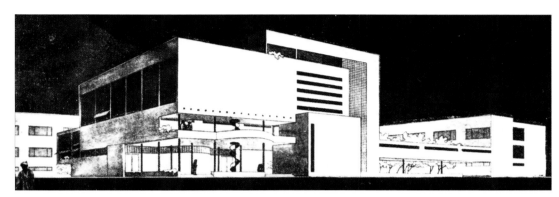

a: Moisei Ginzburg with I Milinis, *competition project for the House of the Kazakh Republic, Alma-Ata, 1928 (first prize: built 1929-31): section through entrance, auditorium and bridge 'court' linking to offices, with mountains behind.*
b: perspective towards entrance.
c-h: six photographs of the model.

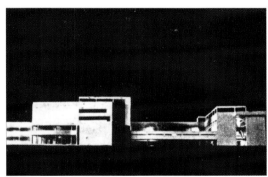

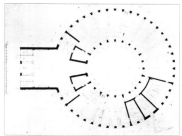

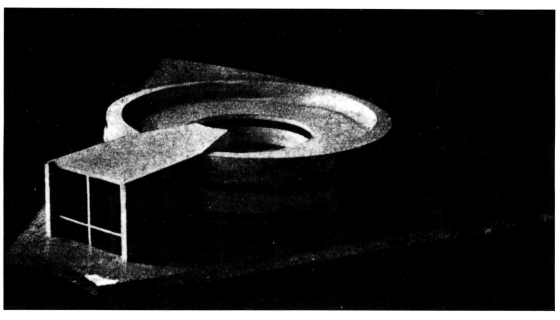

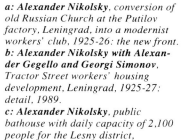

a: Alexander Nikolsky, *conversion of old Russian Church at the Putilov factory, Leningrad, into a modernist workers' club, 1925-26: the new front.*
b: Alexander Nikolsky with Alexander Gegello and Georgi Simonov, *Tractor Street workers' housing development, Leningrad, 1925-27: detail, 1989.*
c: Alexander Nikolsky, *public bathouse with daily capacity of 2,100 people for the Lesny district, Leningrad, 1926-27: plan.*
d, e: *model, exterior wall detail, photograph 1989.*
f: *Secondary School named for the Tenth Anniversary of the Revolution, Leningrad, 1927: detail of teaching block and observatory.*

ПЕРВАЯ ВЫСТАВКА СОВРЕМЕННОЙ АРХИТЕКТУРЫ МОСКВА. ИЮНЬ. ИЮЛЬ. АВГУСТ 1927

1 АРХИТЕКТУРНАЯ МАСТЕРСКАЯ АЛЕКСАНДР НИКОЛЬСКИЙ И. БЕЛ-
ДОВСКИЙ В. ГАЛЬПЕРИН А. КРЕСТИН. КЛУБ С ЗАЛОМ НА 500 ЧЕЛ.
ATELIER A. NIKOLSKY I. BELDOWSKY W. GALPERIN A. KRESTIN. KLUB FÜR 500

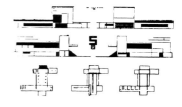

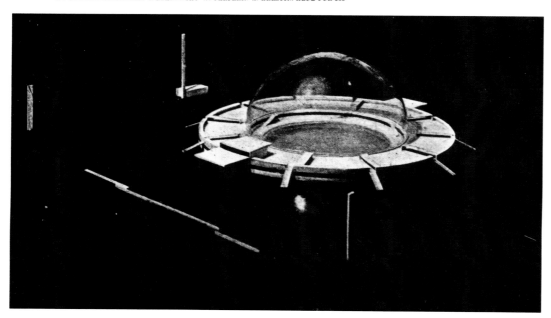

a-c: Alexander Nikolsky with Ivan Beldovskii, Vladimir Galperin and Mikhail Krestin, workers' club with auditorium for 500 people, 1927: view of model, drawing, view of model.
d: Alexander Nikolsky, public bathouse with daily capacity of 4,000 people for the Moscow-Narva District, Leningrad, 1928: model of first project with glazed dome.
e, f: axonometric and plan of second project, as built.

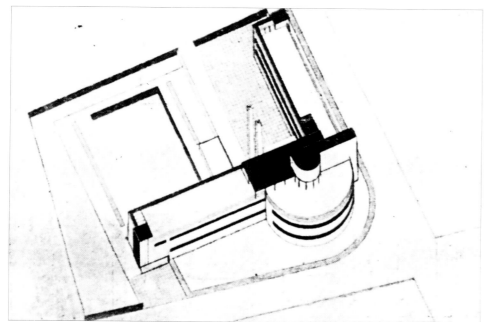

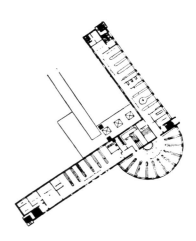

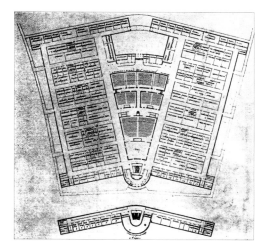

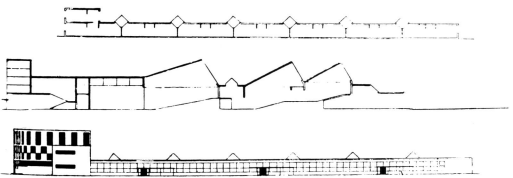

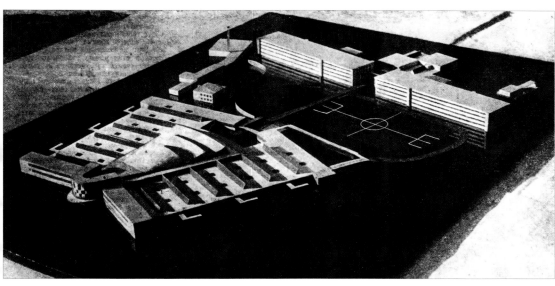

a: Alexander Nikolsky with Lazar Khidekel et al, Higher Cooperative Institute, Moscow, 1930: ground and mezzanine floors of teaching block. b: sections through classrooms, top, and auditoria, centre; side elevation. c: model with teaching accommodation, left and student hostel, right, of whole development. d: isometric.

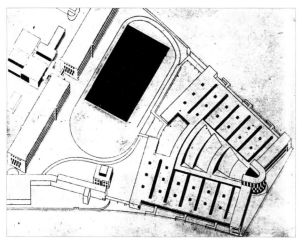

Younger Moscow Constructivists

Andrei Burov

*a: **Andrei Burov,** model dairy breeding complex, built as film set for Eisenstein's 'The General Line' (released 1929 after Stalin's intervention as 'Old and New'), 1926: detail.*
b: Andrei Burov, right, with Sergei Eisenstein, centre, and Le Corbusier, during the latter's visit to Moscow in October 1928.
c-h: Film set for 'The General Line': six stills from the shooting in summer 1926, published in SA 1926, no 5/6.

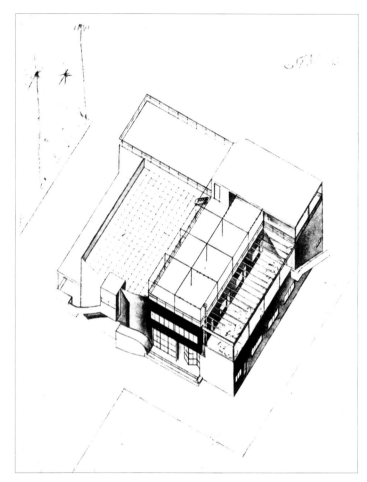

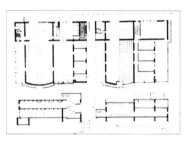

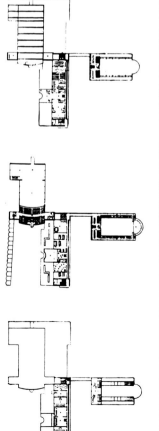

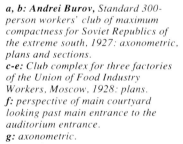

a, b: Andrei Burov, *Standard 300-person workers' club of maximum compactness for Soviet Republics of the extreme south, 1927: axonometric, plans and sections.*
c-e: *Club complex for three factories of the Union of Food Industry Workers, Moscow, 1928: plans.*
f: *perspective of main courtyard looking past main entrance to the auditorium entrance.*
g: *axonometric.*

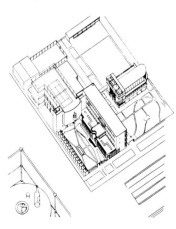

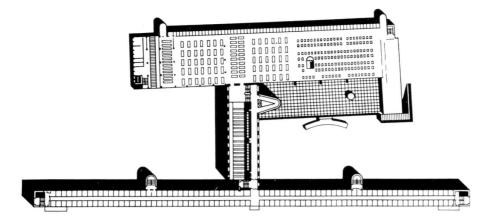

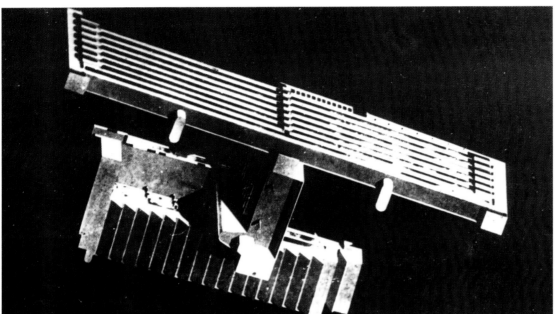

*a: **Ivan Nikolaev**, communal housing complex for trainees and apprentices of the Textile Institute, Moscow, 1929-30: ground-floor plan.*
b: photograph of the model, with T-shape block of minimal individual cabins running north-south, and lower block of communal feeding and recreational facilities to the East.
c: stair tower in north courtyard, photograph 1988.
d: sketches showing 1-4, exterior environments; 5, library; 6, entrance hall; 7, roof terrace outside library; 8, lounge area adjoining dining room; 9, sleeping cabins; 10, orientation, and study carrels on east face of library.

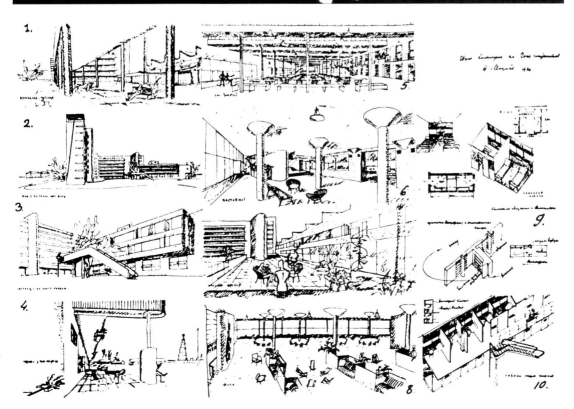

a: Ivan Nikolaev, communal housing complex for trainees and apprentices of the Textile Institute, Moscow, 1929-30: inner corner of main courtyard from porte cochère of main entrance, photograph 1988.
b: photograph during last stages of construction, looking due north into main courtyard.
c: east face of communal block with dining room at ground floor and two floors of library study carrels above.
d-f: Ivan Nikolaev and Anatoly Fisenko under supervision of Alexander Kuznetsov, *All-Union Electrotechnical Institute, Moscow, Central Building, 1928: elevation, perspective, plans and sections from SA 1928 no 3.*
g: The left-hand of this building was the only image representing Soviet modernism in MOMA's 'International Style' exhibition, New York, 1932.

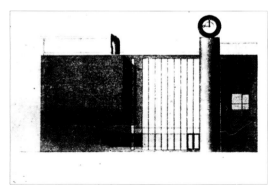

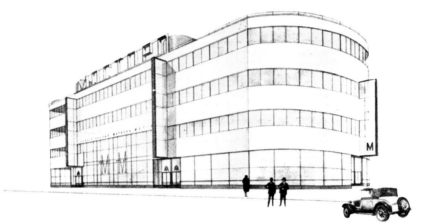

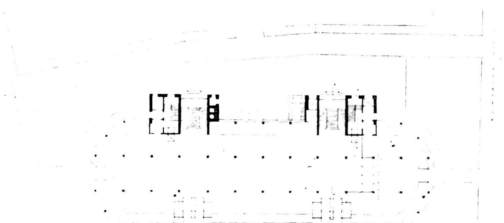

a: Ivan Leonidov, competition project for the Proletarsky District Palace of Culture, Moscow, 1930: elevation and partial section of the 'Mass activities' sector.
b, c: Nikolai Kolli, Mostorg Department Store for the Danilov Market, 1928: perspective, ground-floor plan.
d: Corbusier with Andrei Burov, left, Georgi Golts, centre and Nikolai Kolli, right, during his visit to Moscow in October 1928. Kolli later worked in Paris and Moscow as supervising architect for Corbusier's Tsentrosoyuz building.

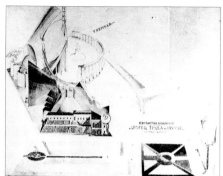

Konstantin Melnikov

a:Konstantin Melnikov, Own house and Studio, Moscow, 1927-29: 'Equal value and evenness of loadings, light, air and heat' – architect's model showing the two interlocking cylindrical forms taken apart.
b: Exterior, with rear cylinder, left, and front cylinder, right, separated by exposed brickwork.
c: Competition project for the Palace of Labour, Moscow, 1923: '8,000 people can all hear a speaker's natural voice' – perspective with Bolshoi Theatre, left.
d: Competition project for model workers housing, Moscow, 1922-23, first stage design: 'Every dwelling in a three-storeyed complex is like a free-standing villa' – typical single sheet with all drawings.
e: New Sukharev Market, Moscow, 1924-26: timber floor frames laid out on site as first stage of construction.
f:'2,000 small traders all have corner sites' – the market in operation, photograph of the mid-twenties by Rodchenko.

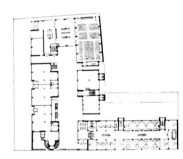

*a, b: **Ilia Golosov,** competition project for the headquarters of the Russo-German Trading Company, Russgetorg, Moscow, 1926: perspective, ground-floor plan.*
c: Competition project for the Lenin House of the People, Ivanovo-Voznesensk, 1924: perspective.
d: Teaching diagrams on themes of rhythm, rhythms of masses, proportions, horizontal movement of architectural masses, relationships of vertical and horizontal movement of masses etc, c1922.

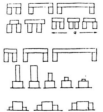
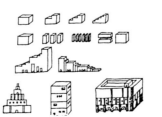

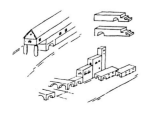
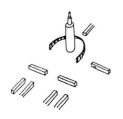
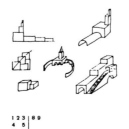
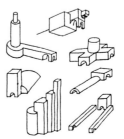

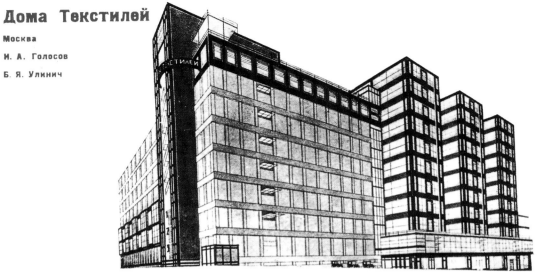

Проект
Дома Текстилей

Москва

И. А. Голосов

Б. Я. Улинич

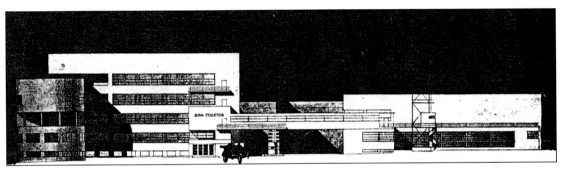

a: Ilia Golosov with Boris Ulinich:
competition project for the House of
Textiles, Moscow, 1925: perspective.
b: Ilia Golosov: competition project for
the House of Soviets, Khabarovsk, 1928
(built 1928-30): elevation.
c, d: Competition project for the Palace
of Labour, Moscow, 1923: elevations.
e: Electrobank building competition
project, Moscow, 1926: perspective.

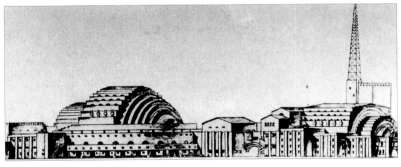

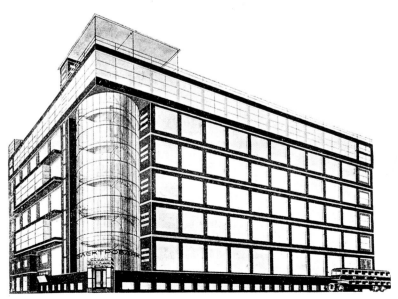

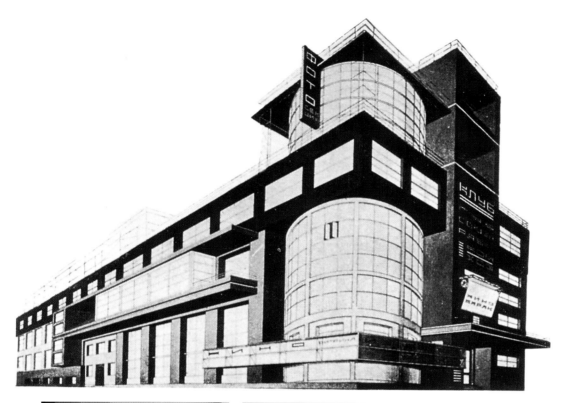

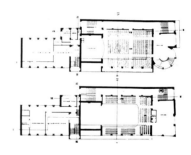

*a: **Ilia Golosov**, Zuev workers' club, Moscow, 1927-29: perspective.*
b: interior view, corner stair rising from first to second floor, photograph 1989.
c: corner view, photograph 1989.
d: ground and first-floor plans.
e: corner stair rising from ground to first floor, photograph 1989.

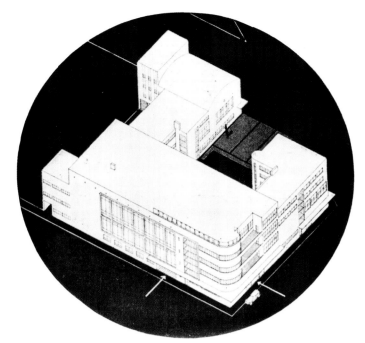

a, b: Grigorii Barkhin, *First prize-winning project for the State Bank in Novosibirsk, 1929: isometric of whole complex, perspective.*
c: *illustration of a composite wall construction from his book* Rabochii dom i rabochii poselok-sad (The Worker's House and the Worker's Garden Settlement), *Moscow 1922.*
d, e: *State Bank in Novosibirsk: ground and second-floor plan.*

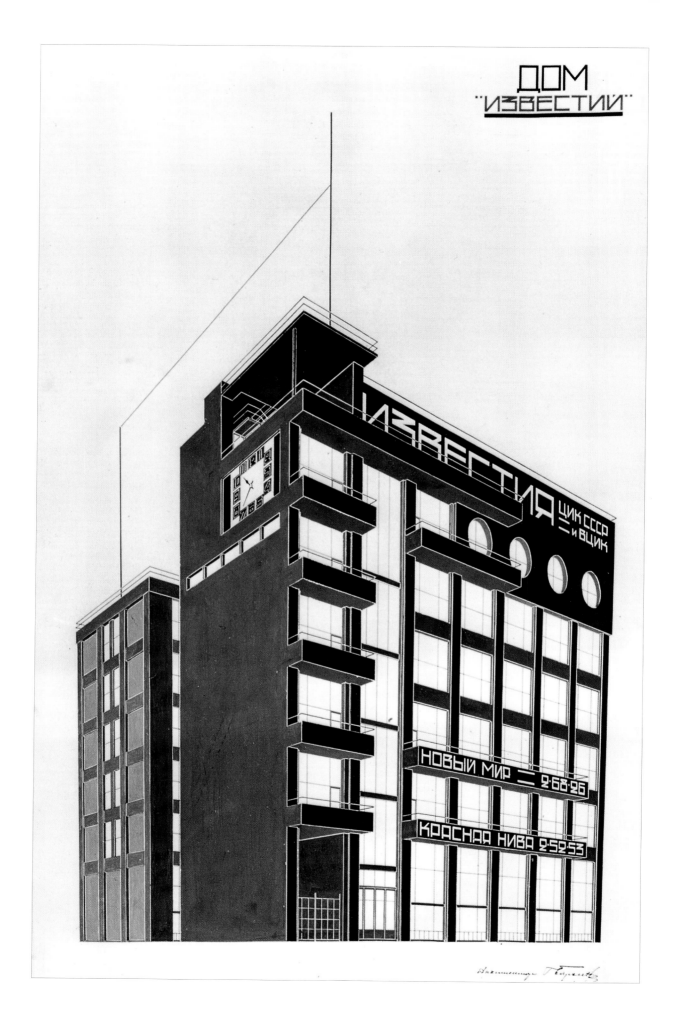

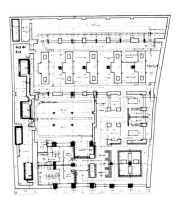

a: **Grigorii Barkhin:** editorial and production building for the Central Committee newspaper, Izvestiia, and its associated periodicals, Moscow, 1925-27: perspective.
b: exterior detail at time of completion.
c, d: interior views of circulation space.
e: photograph soon after completion, showing surrounding city.
f: basement plan with staff facilities and materials stores.
g: Gynaecological sanatorium at Saki, Crimea, 1927 (built 1928-30): main elevation.
h: isometric of whole complex.

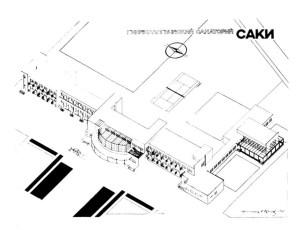

Velikovsky
Kuznetsov
Golosov

Boris Velikovsky

a: Boris Velikovsky with Mikhail Barshch, Georgii Vegman and Maria Gaken, Headquarters for the State Trading Organisation, Gostorg, Moscow, 1925-27: perspective of original scheme with central tower, later prohibited by height legislation.
b: Main elevation soon after completion.
c: Side elevation with what Alfred Barr, Director of MOMA, New York, described in 1927 as 'steamboat balconies', photograph, 1988.
d: view of central circulation space.
e: Concrete frame under construction.

Boris Velikovsky
Panteleimon Golosov

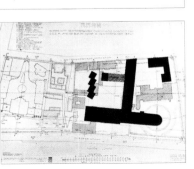

*a: Boris Velikovsky, workers'
housing, Moscow, 1925: photograph
soon after completion.*
*b: Boris Velikovsky with Alexander
and Viktor Vesnin, apartment and
commercial building for IE Kuznetsov,
Moscow, 1910: photograph, 1985.*
*c, d: Panteleimon Golosov, competi-
tion project for the Lenin Library,
Moscow, 1928: perspective, site plan.*

75

ВЭИ

ВСЕСОЮЗНЫЙ ЭЛЕКТРОТЕХНИЧЕСКИЙ ИНСТИТУТ

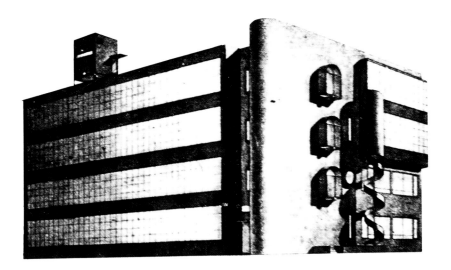

*a, b: **Alexander Kuznetsov with V and G Movchan, Ivan Nikolaev and Anatoly Fisenko,** All Union Electrotechnical Institute, Moscow, 1928-30: two photographs at final stages of completion, published in SA 1929.*
*c: **Alexander Kuznetsov,** Moscow Textile Institute, Wool Laboratory, 1926: perspective.*
d: Headquarters of the Russian Polytechnical Society, Moscow, 1904-06: main elevation, photograph, 1987.
e: Studio building for the Stroganov College of Applied Arts, Moscow, 1913-14: entrance at angle of courtyard.

Leningraders

Alexander Gegello

*a, b: **Alexei Shchusev,** competition project for the Central Telegraph, Moscow, 1926: perspective, ground-floor plan.*
c: Competition project for the Ukrainian House of Industry, Kharkov, 1925: perspective of whole complex.
d: perspective of courtyard.

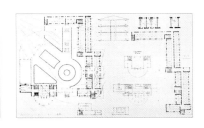

a: Alexei Shchusev, *hotel-sanatorium in new Matsesta, Caucasus, 1927-28: rooftop terrace of guest-room block soon after completion.*
b: *perspective.*
c: *Plans and section.*
d: *Main block of guest rooms under construction.*
e, f: *Details of exterior, soon after completion.*

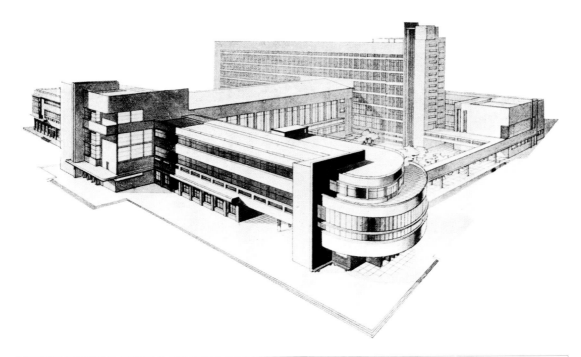

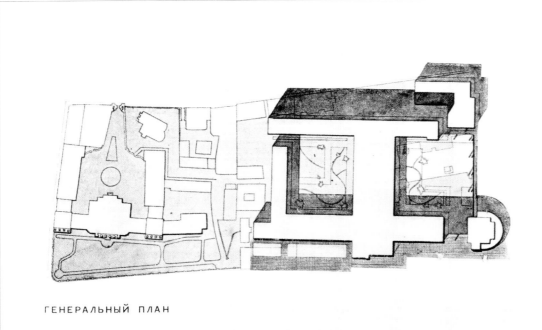

ГЕНЕРАЛЬНЫЙ ПЛАН

a: Alexei Shchusev, Competition project for the Lenin Library, Moscow, 1928: perspective view of whole complex.
b: Site plan.
c: Headquarters of Koopinsoyuz, later Commissariat of Agriculture, Moscow, 1928-33: general view, photograph 1985.
d: Corner detail, photograph, 1985.

a: Ivan Zholtovsky, *mansion and business offices for Gavril Tarasov, Moscow, 1909-12: detail of main street elevation.*
b: *Pavilions of the Machine-building Industry, All-Russian Agricultural and Handicraft Industries Exhibition, Moscow, 1923.*
c: Georgi Golts and Alexander Shvidkovsky, *project for a bank in Novosibirsk, 1926: entrance hall.*

a, b: Ivan Zholtovsky with Sergei Kozhin, *Boiler House of the Moscow Central Power Station, 1927: perspective, site photograph.*
c: Ivan Zholtovsky, *State Bank building, Moscow, 1927-29: detail, photograph 1987.*
d: Ivan Zholtovsky, *project for rebuilding of the Soviet State Bank, Moscow, 1927. Page of attack on the '4 000 000 ruble' affirmed project from the Constructivists' journal SA, no 2, including press cutting from Mossoviet's* Stroitel'stvo Moskvy *September 1927. The Constructivists recognise it as being of significantly higher architectural quality than current attempts to produce a 'monumental modernism', but to them it is precisely its quality which makes the official decision to approve this project 'particularly dangerous to our society', for 'Zholtovsky attempts to justify his complete alienation from our time and epoch by a philosophy of imperishable form and by the quality of his restorationist products.' In their view, this is 'the practical propagation of the ideology of passeists'. It is a 'negative attempt to tie the Soviet Union to principles from the Italian Renaissance and outlived forms of the XV and XVI centuries', by one 'who does not believe in the truths of his own epoch and has not the creative capacity to create its new values'.*

a, b: Georgi Golts, Sergei Kozhin and Mikhail Parusnikov, cotton-spinning factory at Ivanteevka for the Moscow Knitwear Trust, 1928-29: perspective, entrance hall.
c, d: Georgi Golts and Mikhail Parusnikov, boiler house at the Kiev Power Station, 1929: perspective of main street.
e: main structural frame under construction.

a: **Ivan Fomin**, *New Petersburg Apartment Housing development, St Petersburg, 1912: detail of elevation.*
b: *Competition project for the Soviet Pavilion at the 1925 Exposition des Arts Decoratifs, Paris, 1924: end elevation.*
c, d: *New Campus for the Polytechnical Institute at Ivanovo-Voznesensk, 1926-28: perspective of central building, first floor plan of central building.*
e: *Perspective of preparatory faculty for worker entrants (Rabfak).*

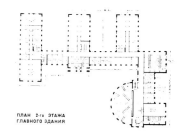

a: Ivan Fomin, Headquarters of the Moscow District (oblast) Executive Committee of the Party, central Moscow, 1928-30: side elevaton onto Stankevich St.
***b, c:** perspective view into main courtyard, photograph soon after completion.*
***d: Ivan Fomin and MI Roslavlev,** Sanatorium named for AA Smirnov, Zheleznovodsk, 1929: photograph soon after completion.*
***e: Ivan Fomin and MI Roslavlev,** Sanatorium 'For Industrialisation', Kislovodsk, 1929: photograph soon after completion.*

a: Ivan Fomin with A Ia Langman,
Dinamo Company complex, central
Moscow, 1929-31: Department store and
office block, photograph soon after
completion.
b: elevation onto Dzerzhinskaia Street
(left hand part only partly constructed).
c: covered walk under housing soon after
completion.

a: Ivan Fomin with A Ia Langman,
Dinamo complex, central Moscow:
photograph of 1988 with shop and
offices, left, and housing, right.
b: apartment housing behind department
store, perspective.
c: housing courtyard soon after
completion.

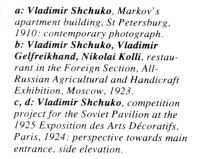

a: Vladimir Shchuko, *Markov's apartment building, St Petersburg, 1910: contemporary photograph.*
b: Vladimir Shchuko, Vladimir Gelfreikhand, Nikolai Kolli, *restaurant in the Foreign Section, All-Russian Agricultural and Handicraft Exhibition, Moscow, 1923.*
c, d: Vladimir Shchuko, *competition project for the Soviet Pavilion at the 1925 Exposition des Arts Décoratifs, Paris, 1924: perspective towards main entrance, side elevation.*

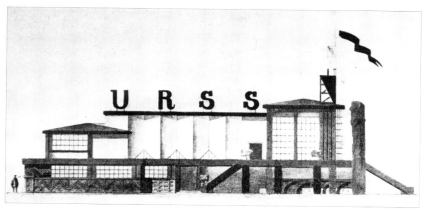

a, b: Vladimir Shchuko and Vladimir Gelfreikh, local transformer station of the Volkhovsky Power Station, Belozerskaia Street, Leningrad, 1926: general view soon after completion, entrance soon after completion.
c: photograph, 1988.
d: Vladimir Shchuko and Vladimir Gelfreikh, Lenin Palace of Culture, Leningrad, c1927: entrance to cinema, photograph, 1988.
e: rear with corner terrace, photograph, 1988.

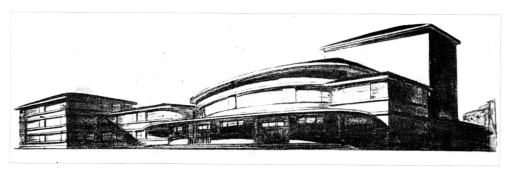

a: Vladimir Shchuko and Vladimir Gelfreikh, project for Textile Workers' Club, Moscow, 1927: perspective.
b: City Theatre in Rostov-on-Don, 1930-31 (built 1932-35): perspective view by day.
c: Perspective view by night.
d: Interior of main auditorium.

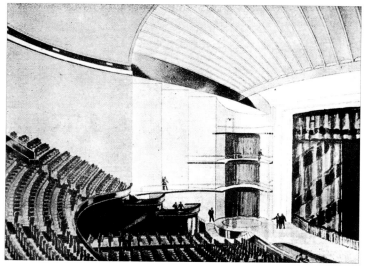

Nikolai Markovnikov

МОСКВА 1925—26 г.
MOSKAU.

a: Nikolai Markovnikov, proposal for a two-storeyed terrace of semi-collectivised workers' housing with communal dining room, 1925: ground and first-floor plans.

b, c: Housing type 60 in timber, for Sokol Garden Settlement, Moscow, 1925-26: photograph soon after completion, ground-floor plan.

d: Housing type 58 in the Gerard blockwork system, for Sokol Garden Settlement, Moscow, 1926: photograph soon after completion.

e: Proposal for a two-storeyed 'Communal house of economic type' compared with the high-rise 'Communal house of the favourite economic type – a model which is without economic foundations and therefore represents an impractical architectural fantasy', 1928.

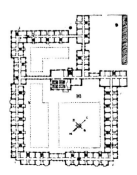
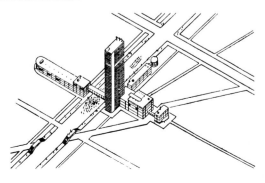

общежитие
профессоров ветинститута
в эривани

А. АГАРОНЯН
О. МАРКАРЯН

72

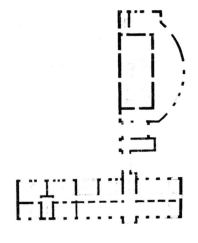

a: A Agoronian and Oganes Markarian, hostel for professors of the Veterinary Institute, Erevan, 1929: photograph soon after completion.
b-d: Karlo Alabian and Mikhael Mazmanian, workers' club for Erevan, 1929: two photographs of model, plan.
e: M Arutchin, furniture for the Club of Building Workers built by Mazmanian, Kochar and Alabian, 1929-31: equipment for art classes; chess tables.
f: Alexander Vlasov and student team, competition project for State Theatre Musical Activities, Kharkov, 1930: perspective of entrance.

OVERLEAF: a: Alexander Vlasov and student team, competition project for State Theatre of Massed Musical Activities, Kharkov, 1930: two photographs of model.

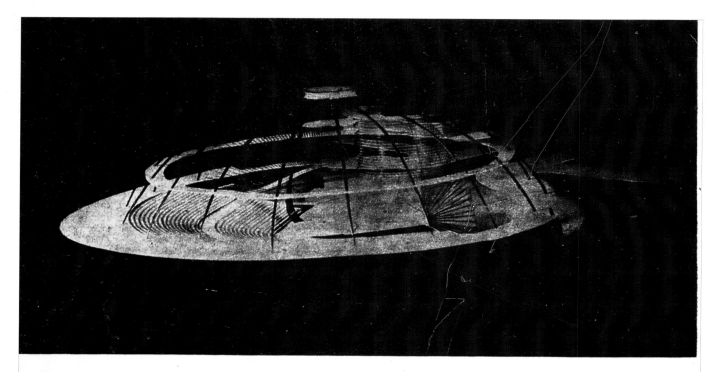

театр
массового
музыкального
действа
в харькове

ВОПРА

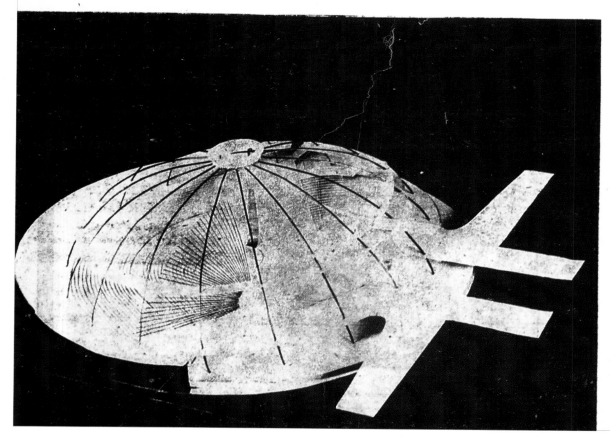